Running Injury

The Ultimate Guide to Running with Confidence as You Age

by

Adrian Ward

Table of Contents

Introduction 1

Chapter One: Understanding The Risk Of Injury For Runners Over 50 5

    The Anatomy And Physiology Of Aging And Its Impact On Running 6
    Understanding The Risk Factors For Injury 7
    Importance Of Injury-Prevention Measures 10

Chapter Two: Types Of Injuries And Their Causes 13

    Overview Of Common Running Injuries For Runners Over 50 14
    The Impact Of Poor Form And Techniques 16
    The Role Of Footwear And Gait In Injury 18
    The Role Of Strength, Flexibility, And Endurance In Injury Prevention 21

Chapter Three: Training For Runners Over 50 24

    Importance Of A Gradual And Progressive Approach To Training 24
    Building A Solid Running Base For Injury Prevention 26
    Understanding The Importance Of Rest And Recovery 30
    The Role Of Cross-Training In Injury Prevention 32
    Incorporating Interval Training And Tempo Runs Into Your Routine 34

Chapter Four: Exercising And Stretching For Injury Prevention 38

    Importance Of Warm-Up And Cool-Down In Injury Prevention 38
    Recommended Warm-Up And Cool-Down Exercises For Runners Over 50 40
    Stretching Vs. Dynamic Stretching 41
    The Importance Of Foam Rolling And Massage 44

Chapter Five: Strength Training For Runners Over 50 48

    Importance Of Strength Training For Injury Prevention 48
    Recommended Strength Training Exercises For Runners Over 50 49
    Incorporating Strength Training Into Your Routine 52

Chapter Six: Nutrition For Running Injury Prevention 57

    Overview Of The Importance Of Proper Nutrition For Runners 57
    Recommended Nutrient-Dense Foods For Runners 58
    Hydration Tips For Runners Over 50 62
    Importance Of Recovery Nutrition 64
    The Role Of Antioxidants In Injury Prevention 64

Chapter Seven: Sleep And Injury Prevention 67

   Overview Of The Importance Of Sleep For Runners 67
   The Impact Of Sleep On Recovery And Performance 68
   Strategies For Improving Sleep Quality 69
   Understanding The Effects Of Sleep Deprivation On Injury Risk 71
   The Role Of Sleep In Injury Prevention And Performance Optimization 72

Chapter Eight: Positive Mental Strength And Injury Prevention 75

   Overview Of The Importance Of Mindset And Mental Health 75
   Understanding The Impact Of Stress On Injury 77
   Mindfulness And Meditation Techniques For Runners 80
   How Do You Meditate While Running? 82
   3 Techniques For Mindful Running 83
   Strategies For Overcoming Mental Blocks And Negative Thoughts 84

Chapter Nine: Managing And Preventing Running Injuries 87

   Overview Of Common Treatments For Running Injuries 87
   The Importance Of Early Intervention In Injury Treatment 88
   The Role Of Rehabilitation And Physical Therapy In Injury Prevention 90
   Incorporating Injury-Prevention Measures Into Your Daily Routine 91

Chapter Ten: Staying Motivated And Making Running A Lifestyle 96

   Overview Of The Importance Of Staying Motivated 96
   Setting Realistic And Achievable Goals 98
   Finding Support System And Accountability Partners 101
   How To Make Running A Lifestyle 102

Conclusion 104

References 106

INTRODUCTION

I love running. I was in my late forties and had been running for most parts of my life. I adore how it made me feel because of how it supported my efforts to maintain my fitness. I was pleased with myself for being able to run several miles every day without any issues.

But as I got closer to my 50s, I started to see some changes. My knees began to hurt, and my legs felt heavier. I noticed that with each run, I was getting increasingly exhausted. Even though I tried to ignore it, the discomfort and pain persisted. When I eventually made an appointment with my doctor, he informed me that I was experiencing the effects of aging and that I needed to slow down.

I was inconsolable because I enjoy running, so I didn't want to stop. I started looking into how to avoid injuries after 50 and found a wealth of advice.

I discovered the value of healthy eating and the necessity of stretching before and after every run. I began increasing my protein, good fats, and water intake to help lessen the strain on my knees; I also started to concentrate on strengthening my legs and hips.

I could immediately tell the difference. My knees no longer hurt, and I felt more light-footed. I ran longer and farther than I ever imagined I could. I was injury-free and feeling better than ever, and I could have fun while running once more. I was astounded by the impact on my life.

After that day, I began to think it was feasible to run injury-free after age 50. I've shared my story with anyone who would listen, and I've always been impressed by its beneficial effects on others being able to run injury-free after age 50, with a little effort and determination.

I produced this book to share all the advice I picked up along the way.

There is no disputing that as we age, our bodies change with time, even though 50 may be the new 40. Usually, something you were able to do a few years ago would now make your muscles feel very sore. However, you don't have to give up just because your 10K training run leaves you feeling really sore (and possibly unable to complete your easy three-mile shakeout run the following day).

Running is a favorite and pleasurable exercise with many advantages for the body and the mind. Running, however, can become increasingly complex and even painful as we age due to our body's changes. It can be hard to deal with the pains and aches that come with getting older, especially if you've been running for a long time and don't want to stop. For people over the age of 50, this is especially true.

Running is a way of life for many people, not merely exercise. It is a strategy to maintain good health, lessen stress, and enhance overall well-being. With some work and commitment, you can run without injury and feel better than ever. The good thing is that you can still run and benefit from running if you're over 50.

This book aims to arm you with the skills and information required to run safely after age 50. Various topics, such as nutrition, flexibility exercises, strength training, and injury prevention, will be covered. We'll also provide a comprehensive guide to help you get started on the road to injury-free running.

Nutrition is a crucial component of injury-free running after the age of 50. Our bodies need different nutrients as we age to function effectively. A balanced diet of protein, good fats, and antioxidants is crucial. We'll provide instructions on how to eat healthily in this book, including details on what you are advised to eat before, during, and after a run. By doing this, you'll be able to maintain your energy levels and lessen your chance of injury.

Another crucial component of injury-free running is stretching. You can reduce your chance of injury, increase flexibility, and lessen muscle tightness by stretching before and after your run. We'll give you a thorough overview of stretching in this book and advice on the best stretches for runners and when to perform them.

Running injury-free after the age of 50 also requires strength training. You can lessen the strain on your knees and enhance your performance by strengthening your legs, hips, and core. We'll advise you on strength training for runners in this book, along with details on the most effective exercises.

When it comes to running injury-free after age 50, injury prevention is essential. This entails giving yourself enough time to warm up properly before your run, donning the proper gear, and gradually increasing your mileage. We will provide a thorough overview of injury prevention in this book, along with advice on keeping yourself safe from common running injuries and what to do if you get an injury.

It's pretty easy to fall into the trap of believing that losing muscle mass and running speed as you get older is just a natural aspect of aging and that it isn't much you can do to prevent it. And to be quite honest, when I first began my studies, I tended to believe this, but along the line, it turns out that there are many things you can do to slow this process down and that the reduction in running performance need not be severe.

Your path to a happier, healthier, and injury-free life begins here! Running injury-free after the age of 50 is possible with a little bit of work and commitment. Even as you get older, you may benefit from running; many physical and psychological advantages by using the advice provided in this book. So, gather your running shoes, don your cap, and get ready to go injury-free.

CHAPTER 1

UNDERSTANDING THE RISK OF INJURY FOR RUNNERS OVER 50

CHAPTER ONE

UNDERSTANDING THE RISK OF INJURY FOR RUNNERS OVER 50

Running can be a terrific way to increase cardiovascular fitness after age 50, and it's a remarkably efficient approach to maintaining strength and fitness as you age. Running is hard on your muscles and joints, but if you don't modify your training program to meet the demands of your body, it can also result in injury. You can take part in running safely if you learn how to begin and maintain it at 50 (and beyond!).

Even though some critics would assert that running is neither healthy nor safe for those in their 50s, this age group continues to enjoy the activity. The fastest-growing age category in the sport is "Masters Runners," defined as individuals above a particular age, usually 40.

The percentage of Masters runners dramatically grew between 1980 and 2009, according to research that looked at participants in the New York City Marathon. In contrast, the number of finishers under 40 significantly fell.

There are strategies to make your running program enjoyable and successful in your 50s and beyond, regardless of your experience level or whether you're a seasoned runner entering a new age group.

Your muscles, tendons, joints, and bones all impact your body's biomechanics, which describes how your body moves as you run. The functioning of the lungs, heart, and circulatory system are all affected by physiological changes. We see a decline in sprint and endurance performance in Masters Runners resulting from physiological and biomechanical changes.

THE ANATOMY AND PHYSIOLOGY OF AGING AND ITS IMPACT ON RUNNING

Our cardiovascular function naturally declines as we age. The efficiency with which your heart contracts, the rate at which it beats, the efficiency with which your blood circulates throughout your body, and the ease and efficiency with which your muscles absorb oxygen from your blood all affect cardiovascular performance. Particularly during exercise, runners notice a decrease in their maximal heart rate.

Our maximum oxygen uptake (VO2 max) likewise declines. Aerobic capacity or VO2 max is the top pace at which your heart, lungs, and muscles can efficiently use oxygen while you exercise. Better endurance performance is directly correlated with a higher VO2 max.

According to reports, lifetime endurance runners in their 80s have a VO2 max almost twice as high as inactive persons of the same age! However, exercising can significantly slow this VO2 max reduction! This is crucial since aging-related declines in VO2 max increase substantially the likelihood of developing chronic illnesses.

In studies that compared highly trained senior runners with highly trained young runners, they discovered that between the ages of 30 and 70, their VO2 max declined by almost 7% every decade.

The VO2 max of older runners who continued to train at high volumes and intensities over time decreased less than that of their contemporaries who trained at lower volumes and intensities.

Unlike endurance athletes, Sprinters don't use oxygen as their primary energy source as they run. They rely on their anaerobic energy system, which uses glycogen as fuel. The by-product of the anaerobic system, lactate, is a substance that may be detected in the blood.

Researchers examined blood lactate levels after competitive 100-, 200-, and 400-meter sprints in a group of male and female masters sprint runners (aged 40 to 88). They discovered sprinters between 70 and 88 had much lower blood lactate concentrations. This suggests that a decline in our capacity to produce energy from anaerobic energy sources may contribute to the decline in sprint performance we observe as we age.

Each of us possesses a mix of fast- and slow-twitch muscle fibers. The fast twitch fibers are employed for sprinting and weightlifting because they create powerful, strong muscle contractions. For endurance exercises, slow-twitch muscle fibers are used. As we age, some of our rapid twitch muscle fibers are replaced by slow twitch ones, contributing to some speed loss.

Our neurological systems oversee how well our muscles contract. Our muscles' number of nerve terminals and the efficiency with which they fire are both impacted by aging.

The good news is that intense strength and resistance training can aid in developing fast-twitch muscle fibers and activating your neurological system.

VO2 max, maximum heart rate, knee and ankle excursion, calf muscle volume, tendon stiffness, fast twitch muscle fibers, ankle power and propulsion force, stride length, increased cadence, and risk of calf strains and Achilles tendinopathy are a few of the changes that occur with age in older runners.

How a runner's biomechanics change as they age

Biomechanics describes how a runner moves their body when running, including their stride length, joint flexion, foot placement, speed, etc. Older runners typically take fewer steps and run more slowly (stride length).

According to experimental studies, a runner should anticipate a 20% reduction in stride length between 20 and 80. This is accompanied by a greater step rate or cadence, which makes sense because you'll have to take quicker steps to maintain your running speed when the steps are shorter.

Their ankles, knees, and hips move through a narrower range of motion and don't oscillate (move) up and down as much. They also tend to have a more flexed knee during foot strikes.

Finally, senior sprinters and endurance runners exhibit lower peak ground reaction and vertical forces. According to researchers, these two elements cause our stride length and pace to decrease as we age.

UNDERSTANDING THE RISK FACTORS FOR INJURY

More people are experiencing injuries as running is becoming a more popular form of exercise. Every year, 19–79% of runners experience injury, and 80–85% of those injuries are brought on by overuse.

Although the evidence is more substantial for some factors than others, research indicates that some factors increase the risk of injury in runners. Understanding these factors is a crucial first step in preventing running injuries since it allows you to take the appropriate precautions to lower your risk. Here, we'll talk about the factors that put runners at risk of injuries.

The four most prevalent risk factors for injury are as follows:

1. Personal factors

Age, sex, height, and other genetic traits are examples of personal factors which cannot be changed. Age as a risk factor is supported by conflicting data, with running experience serving as a better indicator of risk. Beginner runners are more likely to sustain an injury if they are older, overweight or underweight, have a history of injuries, have never run before, or have no running or sporting experience. A greater risk of injury exists for seasoned runners who are older and have a history of injuries.

In general, the research on the connection between gender and running injuries lacks consensus. According to one study, male and female runners have different risk profiles when it comes to running-related injuries. Other personal and lifestyle traits are included in these profiles.

According to some research, older women with a history of endurance running or sports, running on concrete surfaces, and wearing four- to six-month-old running shoes are more likely to get injured. The same study discovered that men were more vulnerable if they had less training, had just started running again, and ran 32-48.7 km or more each week.

The risk ratios revealed for the profiles above statistically have "moderate significance." This indicates that they often fail to anticipate the potential for damage. Other elements are more critical and might offer more clarity when figuring out how to prevent damage.

2. Lifestyle factors

Health and medical history are lifestyle factors, some of which can be changed by changing one's behavior. Smoking, prior injuries, excess weight, and other comorbidities are also some of these factors.

A runner's performance is influenced by their general health, including their diet, fitness level, habits, and amount of sleep they get. The risk of injury correlates with performance since overtraining or consistently poor performance might result in injury.

Our most convincing proof is that previous leg injuries put runners at risk for new injuries. According to a study, a recent leg injury is a risk factor for knee injuries in runners. In the same study, there was proof that any damage to the leg could increase your likelihood of suffering a calf injury. The risk of re-injury was indicated for other, more specific injuries such as Achilles tendinopathy and shin splints.

3. Biomechanical factors

Everything from body form to cadence to stride mechanics is considered a biomechanical factor. To refresh your memory, biomechanics is the study of measurements related to how the body moves. This covers both internal and external structures and forces. In running, we examine the motion, force distribution, and force absorption of the hip, knee, ankle, and foot.

The hip, knee, ankle, and foot joints are among the structures of the leg that are considered in biomechanics. Scientists examine those joints' strength, range of motion, alignment, and angles. A runner's weight, foot strike pattern, and running surface are considered when calculating the forces involved in the running motion.

Combining data from the structures and forces at play during running can provide insight into proper running form. Running injuries can be reduced with appropriate technique, which includes posture, foot strike, cadence (the number of steps per minute), and other factors.

One article examined various running-related structural elements, with findings highlighting the foot and leg structures in particular. It was discovered that injured runners tend to have high, stiff arches. Higher-arched runners may have different ground contact, which could change how the remainder of the body absorbs force.

4. Training factors

Weekly mileage, the training regimen, stretching, and footwear are all essential training variables. Later in this book, we will go into greater detail about these factors. But before that, here are some brief facts:

A runner's risk of injury increases with increased weekly mileage. This is especially true when there is a sharp increase within a short period. Both an increase in running distance and an increase in frequency can lead to excessive mileage. These factors increase the recurring stresses on the leg structures (bones, muscles, ligaments). These structures may malfunction and cause damage if not given the proper rest or conditioning.

Stretching and footwear are both quite divisive subjects. According to research, runners who stretch either after every training session or not at all have a lower chance of injury. Likewise, when considering footwear and orthotics, runners who drastically make changes are more likely to have injuries. This modification can involve wearing minimalist shoes or putting on an orthosis without prior injury history. According to a study that distinguished between various orthoses, runners were less likely to sustain injuries when using custom orthoses as opposed to off-the-shelf ones.

Knowing your body and habits can help you choose the ideal training strategies to make you a safer runner.

IMPORTANCE OF INJURY-PREVENTION MEASURES

Whether you're a professional athlete, weekend warrior, or frequent gym goer, you probably always consider increasing your performance and physical fitness capacity. Nothing is more thrilling in sports and other physical activities than doing something that enhances your appearance and well-being. This is where injury prevention comes into play.

Every physical activity should focus on injury prevention because it helps you reach your training goals and keeps you healthy and secure. Without appropriate preparation, running a marathon can harm your body, just as performing complicated math can harm your brain.

Keeping yourself injury-free requires understanding how to train effectively and safely. Here are some strategies to prevent injuries.

Increase Mileage Gradually

Injury-causing overuse occurs when runners exert themselves too much, too soon, or too quickly. The body requires time to adjust to exercise changes, such as mileage or intensity increases. Increase your weekly training mileage by 5 to 10% per week. Following the 5 percent guideline, you might run 10 miles the first week, 10.5 miles the second, and so on. It is preferable to remain close to the 5 percent restriction if you are healing from an injury or are new to running because going over that limit increases your risk of injury or re-injury. Runners with more experience and a clean medical history can safely train closer to the 10% limit.

Observe your body.

Most running injuries don't come out of anywhere and catch you off guard. They send you signs in the form of pain, discomfort, and lingering pain, but it's up to you to pay attention to them and respond appropriately. To put it simply: Do not run when you are in pain. Stop running and take a few days off from exercise as soon as you feel an injury developing. You can start running gradually after the ache has subsided.

Run half your typical easy-day distance on the fourth day at a much slower pace. Take three days off if you experience unusual pain (pain that intensifies while running or changes how you walk). If you'd prefer, you can swap out gentle walking for a bicycle or another cross-training activity. You could try going a little further the next day if your run went without any pain. Continue reintroducing yourself to your daily routine gradually if you are still pain-free. Whether or not, take an additional three days off before trying it again to see if it is successful. If not, you have two choices: extend your rest time or consult a sports medicine professional.

Strength Training

Strength training helps in maintaining good body alignment when running. The hip and core muscles need to be strengthened. The abductors, adductors, and gluteus maximus in the hips must be strengthened to promote leg stability to the ankles and decrease the risk of a knee injury.

Stretching

Everyone who runs should include stretching in their routine. Running injuries often occur in and around known areas of tightness (most notably the hamstrings and calf muscles).

Preventing injuries when running is crucial, especially if you're preparing for longer races like a half or full marathon. Although no single cause of runner injuries exists, a relatively regular interaction of elements contributes to most runner injuries. Muscle weakness, poor flexibility, training mistakes, using the wrong running shoes, and poor or aberrant biomechanics are among the factors that are often acknowledged.

CHAPTER 2

TYPES OF INJURIES AND THEIR CAUSES

CHAPTER TWO

TYPES OF INJURIES AND THEIR CAUSES

Running is one of the most well-liked activities for improving and maintaining health and staying in shape. In actuality, about 40 million Americans run regularly.

Running is a fantastic way to stay active, but many runners eventually battle with an injury. A sprained ankle or torn muscle might strike suddenly, yet repetitive stress is responsible for more than 80% of running injuries.

Please continue reading to learn more about typical running injuries, their causes, and their usual symptoms.

You may be clocking hundreds or even thousands of kilometers annually if you're a runner like many others. Your muscles, joints, and connective tissue may weaken due to the repetitive impact of all those foot strikes.

The most typical injury areas for runners are their knees, legs, and feet, according to a review of studies published in 2015. The following review details the incidence of running injuries according to the location:

- Lower leg: 9.0 to 32.2 %

- Knees: 7.2 to 50 %

- Upper leg: 3.4 to 38.1 %

- Ankles: 3.9 to 16.6 %

- Foot: 5.7 to 39.3 %

- Hips, pelvis, or groin: 3.3 to 11.5 %

- Lower back: 5.3 to 19.1 %

OVERVIEW OF COMMON RUNNING INJURIES FOR RUNNERS OVER 50

Our bodies change as we age, and injuries also vary with age. When runners are in their 20s, injuries that they experience may not be as frequent or severe as when they are in their 50s or more.

However, once runners enter their Masters' age group, specific injuries manifest more often. Here, we'll discuss the most common running injuries for runners over 50.

Knee Pain

The knee joint is one of older runners' most commonly affected locations. Numerous conditions, such as osteoarthritis, overuse injuries, or muscular imbalances, can result in knee pain. Runners over 50 should be particularly aware of their knee pain and seek medical help if it worsens or becomes persistent.

Plantar Fasciitis

This condition results in pain in the bottom of the foot, usually close to the heel. It is common in senior runners with flat feet or tight calf muscles and is commonly brought on by a repetitive strain injury from overuse. Physical therapy, stretching exercises, and orthotics are all effective treatments for plantar fasciitis.

Shin Splints

Running-related injuries like shin splints hurt the front of the lower thigh. This is often more common in older runners and might result from overuse or a sudden increase in activity. Shin splints can be prevented by stretching and strengthening exercises.

Hip Pain

Runners over 50 often have hip pain, which muscle imbalances, bursitis, or arthritis can bring on. Hip osteoarthritis, which can cause pain and make running more challenging for older runners, is another condition they are more likely to develop. You can treat hip pain with physical therapy, anti-inflammatory drugs, and activities that increase hip strength.

Achilles Tendinitis

The big tendon that joins the calf muscles to the heel bone and generates discomfort in the Achilles tendon is affected by this disorder. Older runners with tight calf muscles or running for a long time often experience this injury. Physical therapy, foam rolling, and stretching can all help lower the risk of Achilles tendonitis.

Groin Pain

Numerous conditions, such as muscular imbalances, overuse injuries, and hip arthritis, can result in groin pain. It is widespread among older runners and can make running challenging. Physical therapy, anti-inflammatory drugs, and hip stability exercises are possible forms of treatment.

Backache

Older runners often have back pain, which muscular imbalances, bad posture, and spinal arthritis can bring on. Running can be challenging for those over 50, so they should be especially aware of back stiffness or discomfort. Exercises for strengthening the core stretches and physical therapy can help relieve back pain.

Stress Fractures

Small fissures in the bones, known as stress fractures, can develop due to repetitive stress or misuse. Older runners with osteoporosis or those running for a long time are more likely to experience them. Rest, immobilization, and physical therapy are all possible forms of treatment.

Runner's Knee

Overuse or muscle imbalances can lead to a runner's knee, a condition that hurts the knee joint. It can make running challenging and is more prevalent among runners over 50. Treatments may include rest, physical therapy, and exercises to increase knee stability.

Tendinitis

Tendons, the powerful fibrous cords that connect muscles to bones, experience pain and inflammation when affected by the disorder known as tendinitis. It can be brought on by overuse or muscular imbalances and is a common injury in older runners. Rest, physical therapy, and anti-inflammatory drugs may all be used as treatments.

We are getting older and have different concerns than we did when we were in our 20s, which is one of the things that most people, runners included, don't want to entertain. It's a tendency to think we can accomplish the same goals as when we were younger, which, like running, I believe we are capable of; it's just that a different strategy is necessary.

Our muscles and tendons lose some of their elastic properties as we age, making us more prone to sprains and tears. Compared to our younger peers who experience "runner's knee" and medial tibial stress syndrome (shin splints) more often. We're all prone to issues and injuries. They merely adjust to the stages of our lives.

The key to staying healthy and running on the road (or trail) is for runners to focus on injury prevention during all stages of life! The good thing is that we can take steps to avoid injury. Strength training, mobility work, and paying attention to proper running technique are a few of them. All of these will be discussed later in this book.

THE IMPACT OF POOR FORM AND TECHNIQUES

Maintaining proper running form helps you train, perform, and stay injury-free. A bad running technique, on the other hand, might ruin your running success and enjoyment, especially during marathon races, where you'll probably log over a million steps!

Here are the causes of your slowness, increased risk of injury, and the advantages of improving your running form. It could be challenging to break lifelong habits but trust me when we say it will be worthwhile.

Looking Down

Your head is extremely heavy. It will force your neck and back out of alignment if it is looking down. It plays a significant role in breathing as well.

Do this: Your chin should be resting on your chest when you lower your head. Take a long, slow breath to let the oxygen fill your lungs. Now take a deep breath and stare straight ahead. Which one was easier? If you look down, avoiding dogs and the dog business may be possible. But by looking forward, you'll be able to spot these threats further in the distance as well as take in the lovely scenery and lovely people around you. Running has many advantages, after all. I'll offer one exception to this rule: if you're running into a strong headwind, you can tilt your head slightly downward to prevent too much wind in your lungs.

Stiff upper body and hunched shoulders

Your entire body will be strained if your shoulders are tense. If your whole body is stressed, your stride length will be shorter, and you will sustain more injuries. Repeat a comparable variation of the trick I described in the paragraph above.

Do this: Pull your shoulders forward in front of you. Take a deep breath in. Do the same when you bring your shoulders back. Which allowed you to breathe in more air? You require oxygen for your muscles. Don't interfere with your lungs' efforts to acquire this; they're working hard!

Wasteful use of arms

I observe many runners who hardly use their arms. The arms are a massive assist in gaining force and momentum, which is one reason why athletes with full or partial arm amputations compete in the Paralympics rather than the Olympics. It isn't a level playing field if you don't use your arms. On the flip side, using your arms correctly is critical. Ensure your arms do not cross over each other and that your shoulders are as immobile as you can keep them while you swing your arms. This helps you preserve energy to run longer.

Leaning Forward from the waist

A lean from the waist is very different from a full-body forward lean. The whole-body lean approach is popular among Kenyans and generally benefits them. One day, a runner confided in me that he leans forward from the waist to increase his aerodynamic efficiency "like a cyclist'." Look at how far a cyclist's foot travels with each revolution; is it maybe 12–15 inches? With each step, your feet ought to advance far further than that!

Your body requires a straight back for a good knee lift and stride length. Do this: Leaning forward at the waist, try to cover more ground as you can in 20 steps. Now walk as far as you can while remaining upright in 20 steps.

Sitting on the hips

Everyone has that one coworker who tries to sneakily accomplish very little work, leaving the rest of you to pick up the burden. Your glutes are that coworker; therefore, you must ensure they don't get away with it! Your other muscles will be forced to work harder due to your weak glutes, which can cause problems with the hip flexors, the IT band, knee pain, and even Achilles tendonitis. Your legs are even held accountable for your glutes' indolence!

Your glutes must be engaged to keep the pelvis stable and the rest of your lower body functioning correctly.

Overstriding

Yes, you should use your legs as much as possible and take long strides, but there is a limit to how long a stride should be. Your shin, knee, hip, and back are experiencing a lot of solid contacts if you notice you're landing on a straight knee or with your foot forward of your knee. Overstriding can also result in running with your feet too high off the ground, slows you down, and forces your body to absorb more force when you hit the ground.

THE ROLE OF FOOTWEAR AND GAIT IN INJURY

Running is one of the best workouts for improving health and extending life. Strengthens the heart, muscles, and bones. Yet, running is quite taxing on the body. It is one of the physically taxing and damaging activities. Our momentum generates forces up to five times our body weight as we run. The shock from this hit travels up our spine and into our feet. This could lead to joint stress and strain, which could eventually cause discomfort and damage. Each time our feet make contact with the ground, our weight-bearing joints must tolerate this strain.

The feet, which serve as the base of our bodies, are essential for absorbing our weight and the intensity of impact while we run. They help us continue to move. Therefore, it's crucial to ensure their safety. And shoes are the best form of protection for your feet. In order to keep your body in the greatest possible shape, the proper footwear can offer you stability and support. As a result, your exercise level will last longer, and your foot health will improve.

Do I Need Running Shoes?

Quick Response: Yes. The only safety gear runners need to prevent injuries is their running shoes. While they might not always help you run faster, they can lessen the pain, repetitive stress, and strain that high-impact exercise places on your joints.

You typically wear footwear for each activity. Tennis shoes are required for playing tennis. Golfers always put on their golf shoes, likewise with running. Even though you can run in anything, wearing the right running shoes will help you avoid pain and injury.

Running shoes are made with a heel that is thicker to absorb impact and a heel-to-toe drop that corresponds to the natural gait cycle of running to complement the natural sensation of your foot. Your feet should feel like an extension of your shoes but with increased protection.

Like car manufacturers, brands produce numerous different makes and models of shoes. You probably know that Toyota and Honda have a variety of automobiles when you think of them. Vans, sedans, SUVs, sports cars, off-road vehicles, and other vehicles are among the many types of vehicles that are produced. Similar to how shoe companies produce different shoes depending on the type of runner you are. This implies that you can find the perfect running shoe.

Do Running Shoes Make a Difference?

The right running shoes do make a difference, yes. They are designed specifically for running and the intense forces it produces. The benefits of wearing the right running shoes are numerous. Fewer foot problems, including blisters, are associated with a snug fit, allowing flexibility and comfort when running. Joint stress is less likely to occur because of the structure's assistance ensuring good running form. The build ensures lifespan and provides the material and padding required to endure impact and repeated stress.

Is Running in Non-Running Shoes Bad?

Your running form, frequency, and distance may all play a role. Most experts advise wearing running shoes or sneakers, while others may be used to wearing less-comfortable footwear. Running frequently in flat-soled footwear, such as Converse, Vans, or dress shoes, might eventually cause irritation and agony.

Running shoes, however important, are not the only factor:

Usually, your gait and biomechanics matter more than the actual shoes. Regardless of your shoes, injuries are possible if you have poor biomechanics and running form. Running and injuries don't go hand in hand; inactive people experience injuries more than runners. Numerous problems that were once primarily attributed to running (such as "runner's knee") are more often caused by improper biomechanics and underlying medical disorders than by running itself (i.e., pre-existing arthritis).

A suitable running shoe is especially crucial if you have biomechanical anomalies or a pre-existing foot condition because they are made for specific foot types and running gaits, promoting proper running form and lessening joint stress. Any running-related biomechanical difficulties can also be resolved by using an orthotic insole.

However, choosing the right running shoes is only one part of the solution; for good biomechanics and injury avoidance, we also need to strengthen and condition our legs and core muscles.

What type of running shoe should I pick?

In the end, it comes down to preference. No one can find the ideal running shoe. Nevertheless, some factors can assist you in limiting your options.

- The surface on which you are running. The terrain you run on affects your body's needs, whether on a rubberized track, grass, gravel, a sidewalk, or the beach. You can choose from cross-training shoes and road running shoes.

- Your foot's shape. Your running gait is influenced by the height of your arch and pronation or how far your ankle rolls in or out. Running shoes fall into one of three categories: neutral, stability, or motion control.

- Health and Injuries: Different amounts of heel drop and cushioning address various ailments and injuries, including rheumatoid arthritis and Achilles tendinitis. Additionally, they will consider your running stride, such as whether you tend to land more firmly on your midfoot or heel as you run.

- Your financial situation. Depending on the brand and type of shoe, running shoes can cost anywhere from $100 and $250 at retail.

- Comfort. In the end, your shoes should be at ease. Ignore the brand, the hype, and the appearance. Because this is your body, put comfort above all else.

More things should be considered while selecting a shoe. Choosing a shoe is a matter of personal preference and depends on your weight, athletic prowess, range of motion, balance, stride patterns, efficiency, and speed.

How long should running shoes last?

A pair of runners should typically last 600–700 kilometers. Shoes can last a few weeks, months, or even years, depending on how frequently you run and how the shoe is constructed. Regularly inspect the midsoles for creases and indications of uneven wear and degeneration. It's also possible that your shoes need to be replaced if you start to feel any new pains.

THE ROLE OF STRENGTH, FLEXIBILITY, AND ENDURANCE IN INJURY PREVENTION

Like most individuals, you perhaps don't give your health much thought until something goes wrong. However, one of the best things you can do for yourself as you age is actively taking steps to maintain your health and to concentrate on preserving your strength, endurance, and flexibility. These three fitness facets are essential for safeguarding your health and independence as you age. Flexibility keeps us limber and lowers our chance of injury, while strength keeps us mobile and independent for an extended period. Here, we will review the significance of these fitness components for runners over 50. We'll also offer advice on maintaining strength, activity level, and flexibility as you age!

The significance of strength for runners over 50

Maintaining physical strength is important at any age but becomes even more significant as we age. We become more prone to injuries as our muscles and bones deteriorate. Additionally, long-term illnesses like arthritis might make daily tasks more challenging. Fortunately, strength training can counteract these consequences of aging and keep us independent and energetic as we age.

Strength training is crucial for adults over 50 to maintain their health and physical activity far into old age and live healthier lives. Strength training benefits are maintaining muscle mass, preventing bone loss, enhancing balance, coordination, and flexibility, and lowering the risk of accidents, slips, and falls. Strength exercises can benefit older persons' cognition and reduce their risk of developing dementia. Additionally, by lowering anxiety and depression, physical training can help enhance mental wellness.

The significance of endurance for runners over 50

Endurance is the capacity for sustained physical or mental exertion. It helps maintain physical health and enhance one's quality of life and mental wellness. It enables us to continue living a full and active life as we age. And as we age, it is even more crucial since it can lessen the effects of age-related decline.

Our metabolism slows down as we age, and we often lose bone density and muscle mass. This might make it challenging to keep a healthy weight and cause exhaustion and low energy levels. However, research has shown that regular exercise can counteract these aging effects. In particular, endurance exercise can help to grow muscle mass, improve cardiovascular health, and speed up metabolism.

Exercise can also enhance cognitive performance, sleep quality, and mental wellness. For people over 50, endurance exercises like cycling, walking, and jogging are beneficial.

The significance of flexibility for runners over 50

Flexibility is often considered a trait only young people and athletes need. However, it's also essential for those over 50 to keep a healthy amount of flexibility. Our muscles stiffen, and our joints gradually become less mobile as we age. This may result in a higher risk of injury. Additionally, stiffness can reduce our range of motion and cause pain.

Regular stretching can help adults over 50 maintain independence by keeping their muscles and joints loose and preventing these age-related issues. Additionally, flexibility exercises can enhance our posture, balance, and coordination and help us maintain our agility far into our senior years.

CHAPTER 3

TRAINING FOR RUNNERS OVER 50

CHAPTER THREE

TRAINING FOR RUNNERS OVER 50

Today's Masters runners are making incredible strides, from weekend warriors keeping up yearly marathon streaks to elite competitors setting previously unheard-of records. If you're a senior runner, we have some training advice to help you keep up a steady pace, avoid injuries, and run for as long as you want.

If you're wondering how to start running at 50 (or older), it's not the most absurd idea. There's no reason to be hesitant to begin your running journey if the last time you were regularly active was in high school or college, whether by playing sports or simply coming to the gym more often.

It is never too late to begin improving your health and fitness. Everyone should follow the same fundamental training principles, but your age and present health should be considered if you want to start running after age 50.

IMPORTANCE OF A GRADUAL AND PROGRESSIVE APPROACH TO TRAINING

A progression run is a beautiful place to start if you're looking for a strategy to change your training week and include some diversity without increasing the load. You can increase your energy and pace through the progression run.

It feels incredible when you get it right, but gauging the appropriate starting pace and session structure can be challenging. In this chapter, you will discover what a progression run is and how it can help us become better, quicker runners.

What is a progression run?

A progression run is a traditional speed-endurance workout that calls for gradually increasing efforts over a predetermined period. Simply put, the run will start easy, build progressively in the effort, and end with a hard effort.

It's an excellent method to add diversity to your training, improve your aerobic system, and run at high-intensity efforts without running the risk of injury.

How can a progression run improve your running?

Progression runs have less impact on the body than a traditional interval or tempo exercise, allowing you to add faster running without becoming more fatigued. They are a sustainable strategy to build endurance while integrating more speed work.

They're wonderful for developing mental fortitude and pacing; they teach you to learn control by delaying the progression portion of the run so you don't become fatigued too quickly.

Thanks to a progression run's enjoyable but challenging nature, you are prepared for race day. The progressive rise in the effort will aid in race day execution.

How to structure a progression run

The easiest way to structure a progression run is by time; you may divide the run into thirds or three equal portions. Take 30 minutes, for instance.

You run for the first ten minutes at a reasonably easy pace. Your effort would have gradually increased to a steady running exertion as you entered the second 10 minutes. Advance to a sustainably hard but comfortable effort for the final 10 minutes.

The most significant thing to remember is gradually to increase your effort over the 30 minutes as you "tighten the screw" toward the end.

You might also include a running progression block in the final 20 minutes of your long runs to spice them up. Increase your effort level from your long-run effort to a comfortably challenging effort every five minutes. This can help you learn how to perform physically and emotionally while having fatigued legs, which is typical throughout the last stretch of a marathon.

If you like running over distance, you could change your progression run to a distance-based one. This could be modified depending on your skill level and level of fitness right now. An illustration of a workout might be a 6 km progression run where you alternate between easy, steady, and pleasantly hard efforts every 2 km. Although the progressive increase will occur at a distance marker, continuing through efforts will still be required.

How often should you incorporate these into training?

Your overall running frequency will determine how often you run a progression session. You can incorporate a progression into your runs once per week if you run three or more times per week and more often if you vary the sessions (a shorter progression run or progressive increase in efforts during a longer run).

Remember that recovery time is when the main training adaptations occur, and you won't grow fitter without it. The trick is to ensure adequate recovery time after each run and before the next session.

The top five suggestions for progression runs are as follows:

- **Comfort:** Running at a low effort throughout the first part will help the body become ready.

- **Control:** Pay attention to gradually progressing through the efforts without commencing the run's progression phase too soon.

- **Race Pace:** Aim to maintain your race pace without overtaxing your body as you near the finish line of the run.

- **Recovery:** Excellent for including fast running without requiring a protracted recovery period after the activity.

- **Variety:** Not every progression run has the same approach! Enjoy your runs and challenge yourself by varying the section lengths; remember that the goal is to finish strongly!

BUILDING A SOLID RUNNING BASE FOR INJURY PREVENTION

We've all heard about base training but probably sought to avoid it. Why, you ask? Base training isn't the most exciting exercise because it emphasizes simple runs with little if any, fluctuations in pace.

Although it isn't the most enjoyable training phase, it is the most important for most coaches.

What Is Base Training?

Any well-designed training program for runners or any athlete starts with base training. Base training is when you gradually increase your aerobic capacity, running your miles at a leisurely, "conversational" pace.

Any structure's foundation must first be sturdy, long-lasting, and self-supporting. A flimsy construction with a potentially unstable foundation will result from a poor foundation.

A runner can advance and improve their performance if their foundation is correctly established. Running too fast without developing a solid base increases the likelihood of plateauing or breaking.

What Purpose Does Base Training Serve?

Base training's primary goal is maximizing your aerobic potential while causing all essential physical changes to prepare you for the next training phase. Before including any anaerobic activity in your training, such as intervals or threshold runs, a strong base must be established.

Let's examine this fundamental goal in greater depth, together with all of its benefits.

1. Decreases Injury Risk

Running is a high-impact activity, and with the proper training, the body is designed to withstand that impact. The body can adapt to the impact by strengthening muscles, bones, and joints with the proper base training (running and strength training).

Base training running is done at a slow pace so that the body can recuperate after each run rather than being tired and having weak legs. This will make you more vulnerable to injury from overuse, including shin splints, runner's knee, stress fractures, and overtraining.

2. Increases the capacity to burn fat and glycogen stores

Your body's glycogen reserves are drained after a longer duration of running. It must turn to consuming fat to obtain energy. Running at a leisurely pace for an extended period will rev up and energize this energy system.

The body gets better at storing glycogen and working the "fat-burning" zone; thus, the body will deal with this " shortfall " more effectively each time.

3. Improves Heart and Vascular Endurance

Your body creates more capillaries surrounding the cells due to more low-intensity exercise, which enables your body to transport more blood and, ultimately, more oxygen to your muscles.

Don't you recall biology in high school? The center of a cell's power is its mitochondria. We can make and consume more energy during running by multiplying our mitochondria and improving their size and strength. Our body also undergoes tremendous mitochondrial adaptation when operating in our base training zone.

Isn't the body fantastic at adjusting to what we need?

4. Strengthens Your Mental Fortitude

A solid block of base training benefits not only your physical body but also your mental health. When we first start running, even short, easy runs seem like a fantastic accomplishment. Both our bodies and our brain must adjust to this challenge.

Examples of Base Training Running Plans

The first few weeks of a running base-building program can resemble this for a beginning 5k runner who can cover that distance while running continuously.

Remember that the weekly rise will be slow because your overall volume shouldn't increase by more than 10% weekly.

Week 1:

- Monday: Strength training session
- Tuesday: Easy run of 20 to 30 minutes
- Wednesday: Strength training session
- Thursday: Easy run of 20 to 30 minutes
- Friday: a 20- to 30-minute XT easy run.

- Saturday: 40 minutes easy run
- Sunday: Rest

Week 2:

- Monday: Strength training session
- Tuesday: Easy run of 22 to 33 minutes
- Wednesday: Strength training session
- Thursday: Easy run of 22 to 33 minutes
- Friday: a 22- to 33-minute XT easy run.
- Saturday: 44 minutes easy run
- Sunday: Rest

As an experienced marathon runner who has just completed a race and the required recuperation period, you will observe that the mileage is the only noticeable change. The length of time has grown, but not the intensity.

Week 1:

- Monday: 50-60 mins easy run + strength training
- Tuesday: 50-60 mins easy run
- Wednesday: 60-70 mins easy run + strength training
- Thursday: 50-60 mins easy run
- Friday: 60 mins XT easy or rest
- Saturday: An easy 90-120 min run
- Sunday: Rest

Week 2:

- Monday: 55-66 mins easy run + strength training
- Tuesday: 55-66 mins easy run
- Wednesday: 66-77 mins easy run + strength training

- Thursday: 55-66 mins easy run
- Friday: 66 mins XT easy or rest
- Saturday: An easy 99-132 min run
- Sunday: Rest

As you can see, the workouts could be more engaging when this base training process is just getting started. However, savor this moment since things will only get trickier from here!

You should take a fitness test every 4-6 weeks to monitor your development.

The mile test, 3k test, and 5k test are a few of the tests you could take. Whatever fitness test you select, ensure it remains constant during the basic training to show progress. Observing how much time you have saved by exercising your aerobic basis is incredibly inspiring.

Even though you probably didn't want to hear this, base training is essential, so take your time and do it right. Later on, you'll thank me.

UNDERSTANDING THE IMPORTANCE OF REST AND RECOVERY

Even though aging is inevitable, staying active can help you feel and look younger. Exercise slows aging by keeping your bones and muscles strong and your heart and lungs healthy. However, aging doesn't mean you should stop caring for yourself after a workout. Remember that whatever your exercise goals are, they are accomplished during recovery time.

See why sometimes it would be preferable to sit back, put the kettle on, and put your feet up rather than lace on your sneakers.

1. You Get Fitter!

Contrary to popular belief, fitness improvements occur when you're not exercising, not when you are. Your body needs to recover to take in your work and allow for the physiological responses to a training stimulus.

2. You Lessen Your Risk of Injury

Your body's tissues sustain minor damage from exercise, and if you don't get enough time to heal between workouts, your body starts to deteriorate. You can lower your risk of developing overuse ailments like tendinitis and stress fractures by building frequent rest days or easy days into your training routine. A recent study based on 446 endurance athletes discovered that athletes had a 5.2-fold increased risk of an overuse injury when they had fewer than two rest days per week during the training season.

3. You Can Mentally Recharge

You can psychologically and physically recover from your training by including a regular rest day or a very easy day. To prevent psychological burnout, it's crucial to "switch off" from training and pursue other hobbies.

4. You can exercise more frequently.

Respecting the value of rest and recovery can lower your risk of injury and reduce the possibility of succumbing to overtraining weariness, allowing you to train more. If you want to improve your running, consistency in your training is likely the most crucial component. Fitness is established over weeks, months, or even years of continuous, hard training; one or two intense workouts do not achieve this.

5. You Can Work Out More

Your ability to recover determines how hard you can train. Your body will adapt to and absorb additional training over time without the risk of overtraining if you give it enough time to rest and recuperate. You'll be able to perform at higher levels as a result.

6. You'll perform better in races.

Many runners need to be made aware that in the last two weeks before a race, there is essentially no fitness to be gained. If you'd like to be at your best during the final week before a race, you should prioritize rest and recovery because it takes at least ten days to two weeks to benefit from any given activity fully. The hard training is done, so shorten your runs and take some time to relax.

7. You Can Periodize Your Exercises.

Even professional sportsmen will admit that maintaining excellent physical condition all year is challenging. Periodizing your training will help you perform at your best. This entails segmenting the year (or many months) into smaller timeframes, each with a different focus. Rest and recovery are crucial components of periodization and should be sprinkled throughout each training block to help you absorb all the training and maximize those crucial fitness improvements.

Remember that taking time off from exercise counts as training, and you should treat it with the same rigor you would treat your more challenging sessions.

THE ROLE OF CROSS-TRAINING IN INJURY PREVENTION

Cross-training is any activity that you do in addition to your primary sport. According to studies, cross-training has many advantages for runners. There are several benefits to cross-training, regardless of your level of experience running marathons.

Benefits of Cross-Training

Cross-training balances your muscle groups by strengthening the muscles not used as much when you run. You can concentrate on body parts not used as much while running, like your upper body.

You can keep up with or even raise your cardiovascular fitness with cross-training. Since many cross-training exercises are excellent cardiovascular exercises, they build on similar benefits to running.

You can lessen your risk of injury by balancing your weaker and stronger muscles. Exercises with low impacts, such as swimming or water running (aqua jogging), can be done as a cross-training activity to help runners' joints, which are often sore, feel less stressed.

Even the most ardent runner will ultimately become exhausted from running every day. You can avoid growing tired of running by mixing up your workouts with cross-training. Cross-training allows athletes to take a much-needed mental vacation from their activity, which is crucial for anyone training for marathons or other long-distance races.

With specific injuries, you can keep training if you give them enough time to heal. Injured runners may occasionally be advised by their doctors to stop running while they recover. However, some injuries may allow you to keep up your cross-training. Athletes who cross-train can keep up their fitness and cope better with the frustration and sadness of being sidelined.

When Is the Best Time to Cross-Train?

Your level of cross-training will depend on how you feel physically and emotionally. Add two to three days of cross-training to your three to four days of jogging if you are a leisure runner.

If you compete in running and run four to six days per week, you can replace an easy run or a rest day with a low-intensity cross-training session one to two days per week. For runners who are on the road and may not be able to run outside or on a treadmill but have access to other sports, cross-training can be significant.

Both novice and seasoned runners may suffer times during their training when they don't feel motivated to run. Cross-training is a fantastic strategy to get through those demotivating periods. It can be easier to get motivated to start running again if you take a few days off each week to engage in another activity.

There are numerous alternatives for cross-training exercises. Depending on availability and preference, pick one (or a few).

- Water Running
- Swimming
- Cycling or Spinning
- Pilates
- Elliptical Training
- Cross-Country Skiing
- Walking
- Strength Training
- Rowing
- Yoga

Cross-training enables runners to increase their workout without running into overuse issues. Additionally, it improves other aspects of your fitness, such as your cardiovascular system, core stability, and muscle and flexibility.

Building muscle can help prevent common running injuries through strength training. Exercises like yoga, Pilates, and walking can help you feel less stressed and speed up your recovery. Pick cross-training activities that you enjoy and will help you maintain a positive relationship with fitness and exercise.

INCORPORATING INTERVAL TRAINING AND TEMPO RUNS INTO YOUR ROUTINE

All of your training ultimately serves to increase your "race pace." You can use various training techniques to encourage specific physiological adaptations to increase your speed endurance, aerobic capacity, lactate threshold, and mental strength. The most effective ways to improve your "race pace" are interval training and tempo workouts. We must emphasize the physiological adaptations caused by exercising at these intensities to understand the various advantages of these sessions.

Interval Training

Interval sessions are when you repeatedly put forth solid and challenging efforts followed by lengths of easy recovery. As you exhaust your muscular glycogen stores during the brief bursts, these sessions strain aerobic and anaerobic energy systems. The aerobic energy system recharges the muscles by turning stored carbohydrates into energy using oxygen. The intervals will be longer than your anaerobic threshold and last from 10 seconds to four or five minutes. The length of time you spend between sets will also change depending on the goals of your training sessions. Interval training has been demonstrated to boost your maximum aerobic capacity, increase the volume of your stroke, and enhance the capacity and functionality of your mitochondria.

Your stride length and cadence will increase due to these exercises, improving the efficiency of your leg turnover and movement. The more often you undertake these exercises, the more your body will adjust to the stress and be able to recover more quickly, even if they first feel incredibly draining and can take a few days to recover from.

Always work out at a faster tempo than the one you want to race at. Your ability to judge what pace you can maintain will improve the more interval training you finish. Finding a quicker tempo, you can keep up with throughout the set without fading on the last few reps is essential for successful interval training.

Short, fast interval training

Shorter, faster intervals will work best if you aim to improve your 5–10 km timings. You want to train your body to handle stress at these maximum intensities to improve your ability to tolerate and remove lactate buildup. Examples of sessions are:

- 10 x 200 meters with 30s of recovery
- 10 x 800 meters with a 60-second recovery
- 6 x 1 km with a 90-second recovery

Interval training for a longer distance

If you aim to develop long-distance running, you will gain most from longer duration intervals, where you want to push that anaerobic endurance. A few examples of sessions are:

- 6 x 1km with a 3-minute break
- 6 x 3 km with a 2-minute break
- 5 × 5 km with a 3-minute break

Responsive shoes give you that extra energy return to propel you forward for optimum performance throughout intense activities.

Tempo Training

Tempo runs, also called lactate threshold runs, should be conducted at a pleasantly challenging effort, which means pushing yourself just a bit beyond your comfort level without going all out. The ideal intensity for working out is when you are at your lactate/anaerobic threshold, when lactate production and removal are at their highest levels and are perfectly coordinated. This level of effort often corresponds to 85% of your maximum heart rate or 75% of your maximum aerobic capacity. Moreover, the fastest pace you can maintain for 60 minutes of jogging; sessions typically last 20 to 40 minutes. You shouldn't feel like you're working out in a race at this pace; you should only be able to mumble a few words rather than carry on a conversation.

Your performance will significantly benefit from tempo runs since they teach your body to handle running at higher intensities for extended periods. Several physiological adjustments contribute to this. First, tempo running is the best way to raise your lactate threshold. You can exert more effort for longer since it makes your body more effective at buffering lactate. Running at a tempo requires you to train outside your comfort zone, which will significantly help you on race day. It also enables you to develop mental toughness. As you must run at higher intensities without stopping, it is the most specific to racing. These sessions also make up a significant portion of your training load.

Your pace will vary slightly during tempo sessions depending on how long the session lasts. The general rule of thumb with tempo running is to keep up a pace you can sustain for an hour. This is often 20 to 40 seconds slower than your 5 km speed.

Tempo sessions for shorter distances

Including a recovery segment in your tempo session is also helpful. This is where you reduce the intensity by around 10% and give your body 500 meters to recover. This enables you to sustain the session's intensity and mentally divide the session into smaller chunks. Anywhere between 3 and 10 kilometers of tempo exertion would make up a regular workout. Like interval training, shorter tempo efforts will positively influence your performance if you train for shorter distances. For instance:

- 4/5 x 1 km tempo effort with a 0.5 km rest between sets.

- 44/5 x 1-mile tempo effort with a 0.5 km recovery in between.

Tempo sessions for long distances

Longer tempo efforts are advised if you are training for longer distances. 10 to 20 to 30 kilometers would often be covered throughout a session. Examples include:

- 6 x 3km tempo effort with 0.5 km rest between sets.

- 2 x 10/15km with a 0.5 km recovery in between sets

CHAPTER 4

EXERCISING AND STRETCHING FOR INJURY PREVENTION

CHAPTER FOUR

EXERCISING AND STRETCHING FOR INJURY PREVENTION

Stretching is a fantastic strategy to reduce aches, loosen up muscles, and relax your joints as you age. People slow down as they get older, which is conventional information.

Daily tasks like getting out of bed and getting up from a chair become more challenging. A loss of muscle flexibility and strength often brings on these restrictions.

Flexibility refers to a person's capacity to lengthen and stretch their muscles and tendons in reaction to movement, enabling a joint to move through its range of motion. To preserve flexibility, it's crucial to incorporate a decent stretching practice into your everyday routine.

As you age, maintaining flexibility with stretches for your neck, arms, back, hips, and legs can keep you limber for everything life offers.

IMPORTANCE OF WARM-UP AND COOL-DOWN IN INJURY PREVENTION

Consider performing a quick warmup before you hit the running trails or get on the elliptical machine. A few minutes may be added to your exercise regimen for a warm-up and cool-down, but they could also help to lessen the strain on your heart and other muscles. Additionally, consider finishing your workout with a short cool-down period.

Warm-up exercises include gentle bike riding or light jogging. By increasing blood flow to your muscles and raising body temperature before exercise, warming up gets your cardiovascular system ready for physical activity. Additionally, it helps to reduce the chance of injury because your muscles will be less stressed during your workout if they have had enough time to warm up. Additionally, it lessens muscle soreness.

Your heart rate and blood pressure should gradually return to pre-exercise levels as you cool down after your workout. Your heart rate has been pumping much faster than usual during your workout, so it's crucial to gradually slow it down rather than halting all movement immediately. Additionally, cooling down helps control blood flow, which is essential to seniors who engage in endurance activities like long-distance running. Gradually slow down your activity rate for the final 10 minutes of your workout. For instance, if you were running, slow down to a brisk walk for those 10 minutes.

Benefits of Warming Up

Your sports performance will benefit from warming up in the following ways:

- **Increased Blood Flow** – By warming up for 10 minutes with low-intensity activity, you can increase the amount of blood that reaches your skeletal muscles and widen your blood capillaries. One major thing you can do to prepare your muscles for a workout is to increase your blood flow since your blood transports the oxygen required for your muscles to perform.

- **Increased Oxygen Efficiency** – During a warm-up workout, your blood releases oxygen more quickly and at a higher temperature. When exercising, your muscles require more oxygen, so it's critical to increase the oxygen's availability through a warm-up activity.

- **Quicker Muscle Contraction/Relaxation** – Getting warm during exercise boosts body temperature, which enhances nerve conduction and muscle metabolism. The outcome? Your muscles will work more quickly and effectively.

- **Injury Prevention -** By increasing blood flow to your muscles and loosening your joints, warming up helps you avoid injuries by reducing the likelihood that your muscles will rip, tear, or twist unsafely while you exercise. Stretching also aids in preparing your muscles for the upcoming physical activity.

- **Mental Preparation -** As you warm up, your brain will focus on your body and physical activity. Your training session will continue with this focus, which will help develop your technique, coordination, and skill.

Benefits of Cooling Down

- Recovery - Lactic acid accumulates in your system after a vigorous workout, and it takes time for your body to eliminate it. Stretching and other cooling-down exercises can help release and remove lactic acid, hastening your body's post-workout recuperation.

- DOMS (Delayed Onset Muscle Soreness) reduction - While some muscle soreness is following regular exercise, a lot of DOMS is extremely uncomfortable and can discourage you from working out again. According to California State University research, cycling at a moderate intensity after strength training reduced DOMS. It keeps you more comfortable and enables your body to recover before your next session by reducing excessive muscular soreness after exercise.

RECOMMENDED WARM-UP AND COOL-DOWN EXERCISES FOR RUNNERS OVER 50

You should warm up and cool down before each of your runs. These two bookends to your run will help your muscle prepare for peak performance and post-workout recovery.

How to Warm Up for Running

Follow these steps to warm up for your run:

- Warm up for your run by doing five to ten minutes of light aerobic activity. You can warm up for a run by walking briskly, marching, jogging slowly, or riding a stationary bike. Don't rush through your warm-up.

- If you enjoy dynamic stretches or exercises before your run, perform walking lunges, jumping jacks, or opposing toe touches.

- Start the run. Start jogging gently and increase your speed over time rather than racing. It's easy to start fast; this is part of knowing how fast to run. Your breathing ought to be quite effortless. Slow down if you start to feel out of breath.

- When you start your run, pay close attention to your running form and posture. Before you accelerate, be sure you are employing the optimal approach.

How to Cool Down Correctly

Follow these instructions after your run:

- After your run, cool down by strolling or jogging slowly for five to ten minutes. Your respiration and heart rate should gradually return to normal.

- Rehydrate your body by drinking water or a drink that contains electrolytes.

STRETCHING VS. DYNAMIC STRETCHING

Stretching is essential to playing or practicing a sport for serious and less serious players. Stretching increases the range of flexibility and motion while reducing stiffness, which lengthens your soft tissues like muscles and ligaments. Additionally, it can help with post-exercise pain and improve your performance in your sport while lowering your chance of injury.

Stretching can be divided into two categories: static stretches and dynamic stretches. Static stretches are those in which you remain standing, sitting, or lying still for up to 45 seconds at a time. Controlled motions, known as dynamic stretches, prepare your muscles, ligaments, and other soft tissues for action and safety.

These should be used at various points throughout your workout because they serve different objectives.

Dynamic Stretching

During the stretch, you actively contract your muscles and rotate your joints through their complete range of motion. These practical and athletic movements aid in raising muscle warmth and lowering stiffness. This type of stretching improves acceleration, speed, and agility.

Before each athletic event, whether competitive or not, you should warm up with dynamic stretches. Approximately 5 to 10 minutes of low- to moderate-intensity cycling, jogging, or swimming, followed by dynamic stretches, should make up a thorough sports warm-up.

Here are some types of dynamic stretching.

1. Torso twist

Maintaining spine flexibility is advantageous for players participating in throwing and striking sports like football, baseball, tennis, hockey, and lacrosse. Stand with your back to the wall, your arms by your sides with a 90-degree bend, and your feet shoulder-width apart. Maintain the same alignment of your feet while slowly rotating. Maintaining spine flexibility is advantageous for players participating in throwing and striking sports like football, baseball, tennis, hockey, and lacrosse.

2. Walking lunge

Standing with your arms at your sides, lunge forward while keeping your front knee parallel to your ankle and hip and lowering your back knee without bringing it into contact with the floor. Avoid letting your front knee cross your front toes. Letting go of the back leg, stride forward with the other leg while lunging. Keep your abdominal muscles active throughout the exercise to prevent your back from arching. All athletes can benefit from this, but track and field athletes, soccer players, rugby players, and football players, since it helps stretch the hamstring, gluteus, and hip flexor muscles.

3. Leg swing

Standing on one leg, slowly and deliberately swing the opposite leg through its complete range of motion in front of and behind you. To keep your back from arching, contract your abdominal muscles. The hamstrings and hip flexors benefit from this stretch as they get ready for jogging.

Static Stretching

Static stretching needs you to move a muscle as far as it will go without hurting, then hold that position for 25 to 40 seconds. It is quite efficient to improve flexibility in this way. Static stretches should be performed twice to three times each.

To help prevent injury, do static stretches in your cool-down routine. Your risk of injury can be decreased by using static stretching as part of your maintenance stretching routine.

However, performing static stretches as part of your warm-up before an athletic competition may hinder your performance. This is because static stretching could make it difficult for your body to respond rapidly. This condition could persist for up to two hours when engaging in vertical leaps, brief sprints, balancing, and response times.

Here are a few static stretch examples to try out.

1. Posterior capsule stretch

Relax your shoulders, cross one arm over the other, holding it just above the elbow, and slowly draw it toward your body. All players in throwing sports like football, baseball, and basketball can benefit significantly from this back-of-the-shoulder stretch.

2. Hamstring stretch

Your hips and feet should be pointed forward as you prop one leg up on a low stool. When you feel a stretch in the back of your thigh, lean forward from the hips while maintaining a level back and a straight knee. Hamstring stretches might help you avoid injuries when running.

3. Quadriceps stretch

From the same side, grab one ankle with your hand. To keep your back from hunching, contract your stomach muscles. Bring your ankle toward your butt, extend your thigh backward, and bend your knee. By keeping your ankle in line with your hip rather than tilted outward or inward toward your body, you can always ensure that your knee remains in alignment with your hip. This stretch should be felt at the front of your thigh. Quadriceps muscles benefit from this stretch.

Use dynamic stretching before working out to warm up your muscles and joints, and concentrate on stretches that match the action you're about to do. Change to lengthier holds with static stretches when it's time for a cool-down because they can increase flexibility and speed up recovery.

Always remember to listen to your body when performing either of these two types of stretches. During a warmup and cool-down, stretching should feel energizing and restful.

THE IMPORTANCE OF FOAM ROLLING AND MASSAGE

A foam roller, often known as a self-massage tool, is a cylindrical piece of foam used to treat muscular stiffness following a workout. Self-myofascial release involves connective tissue (fascia) and muscles (myo). Working away adhesions (also known as tightness) or trigger points (also known as knots) that produce discomfort or soreness is one of the main advantages of foam rolling.

Physical therapists often use foam roller exercises to target muscles all over the body, including the glutes, hamstrings, IT bands (ITB), hip flexors, quadriceps, and calf muscles. Exercises involving foam rolling help the body's tight places and muscular tissue release tension, which helps to prevent injuries, athletic support performance, and improve the soft tissue quality. When carried out correctly, they also help enhance blood flow, supporting overall health and muscle flexibility.

Benefits of Foam Rolling for Runners Over 50

There are several benefits to using a foam roller, regardless of your experience as a runner.

- Adhesions in the thin layer of connective tissue (fascia) surrounding muscles in the body are often linked to sore muscles and back discomfort. • Foam rolling can help muscles heal. Particularly while preparing for a marathon, a foam roller is an excellent recovery tool for self-myofascial release on tight muscles that feels like a deep tissue massage.

- Foam rolling can help shield you from injury. Static stretching is one of the best ways to prevent injuries and should be done after exercise. Include foam roller activities as part of your post-run cool-down to maintain muscle health and prevent shin splints.

- Foam rolling can help with form improvement. You may find it challenging to run with good form if your muscles are tight. Exercises, including foam rolling, boost blood flow to loosen up tense muscles and enhance your running form.

Techniques for Foam Rolling for Runners

Try using these foam rolling techniques while warming up or cooling down after a run.

- **Hamstrings:** Sit on the ground and lay the foam roller under the middle of the backs of your upper legs to foam roll your hamstrings. Put your hands in the back. Lifting your hips off the ground with a push from your hands will allow the roller to apply pressure to your hamstrings. Find a sore place by slowly rolling up and down while applying pressure to your hamstrings from the bottom of your glutes to your knees. Once you've determined which area of the muscle is the most sensitive, apply pressure there with a foam roller for 30 to 90 seconds while relaxing or until the pain subsides.

- **Quadriceps:** Lay down on your stomach and place the foam roller in the center of your thighs to foam roll your quadriceps. As if you are performing a plank, position your forearms in this position. Your feet should be elevated, and your legs should be straight. Roll slowly up and down, covering the quad muscles from your hips to your knees while keeping an appropriate posture. Find the area of your most tender quads by softly rolling that area with the foam roller. Hold that position while relaxing for 30 to 90 seconds or until the soreness fades.

- **Adductors:** Lie face down on a yoga mat to foam roll your adductors. Raise your upper body and forearms as if performing a plank with your lower body in contact with the floor. You can place the foam roller under one of your legs by bending your knee and stretching your leg to the side. The center of your inner thigh is the ideal location for the foam roller. Straighten the leg on the other side. Roll the inner thigh slowly back and forth, covering it until a sore place is found. The most tender area of your adductor can be located by carefully rolling it with the foam roller. Hold that position while relaxing for 30 to 90 seconds or until the discomfort fades. Repeat with the other leg.

- **Iliotibial band (ITB):** Your IT band, also known as the iliotibial band, extends from your hip to your knee. There is a muscle called the TFL muscle at the top of the IT band. Lower back strain might result when it becomes tense. Lie on your side with the side of your hip directly on the foam roller to relax your IT band. Maintain your alignment by keeping your legs extended and your hand directly below your shoulder. Slowly glide the side of your hip along the foam roller using a very small range of motion.

- **Piriformis:** Your gluteus maximus gives your lower back and leg muscles stability and strength. A tiny muscle called the piriformis is found deep within the glute. Place a foam roller horizontally on the floor, sit on top of it, cross your right leg over your left knee, and bend your right knee into the shape of a four to foam roll the piriformis. Keep your right hand supporting you behind you and your left foot firmly on the ground. Roll the whole gluteal surface region by swaying your body from side to side. After that, repeat on the other side.

How to Exercise Safely and Prevent Injury

Proper exercise technique is crucial to maintain the security and efficacy of an exercise program. However, depending on your particular demands, you might need to adapt each exercise to get the best results. Always choose a stretching exercise that enables complete body control during the exercise. Pay special attention to your body when exercising, and stop immediately if you experience any pain or discomfort. If you have a history of health issues, speak to your doctor before you start an exercise program.

Include the appropriate warm-ups, rest, and nutrition into your training regimen to see continual progress and increase body strength. Your capacity to effectively recover from your workouts will ultimately determine your results. Before you work out the same muscle groups again, rest for 24 to 48 hours to give your body enough time to heal.

CHAPTER 5

STRENGTH TRAINING FOR RUNNERS OVER 50

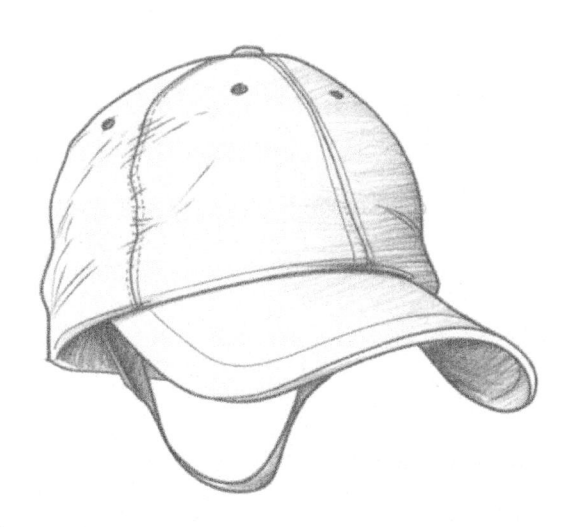

CHAPTER FIVE

STRENGTH TRAINING FOR RUNNERS OVER 50

It's never too late to begin working out; seniors can significantly benefit fitness-wise in many ways. While any form of exercise can be good for your health, strength training is especially crucial for people over 50.

Strength training becomes increasingly crucial as we age since we start to lose muscle mass and bone density.

This chapter will cover the benefits of strength training for seniors and the finest strength training routines for people over 50 (or older.

IMPORTANCE OF STRENGTH TRAINING FOR INJURY PREVENTION

Everyone should engage in strength training, but after the age of 50, it becomes even more essential. Big biceps and flat abs are no longer the focus; instead, the emphasis shifts to maintaining a robust, healthy physique that is less prone to illness and injury.

After age 50, your body benefits from strength training in the following ways:

- **Increases bone density:** Every year, unexpected falls send thousands of elderly patients to the hospital. An 8-year-old can resume playing in 8 weeks after getting his arm cast. A person in their 80s is not quite as fortunate. Broken bones can have terrible repercussions. Strength training is beneficial.

- **Increases muscle mass:** You won't become the Incredible Hulk. It implies that you are a strong, sturdy person capable of pushing your lawnmower, lifting your groceries, and picking yourself up when they fall.

- **Reduces body fat:** Too much body fat is unhealthy for anyone, regardless of age. Keeping a healthy weight is crucial, especially if you want to avoid the many diseases that affect seniors.

- **Enhances mental health:** As people become older, their chances of developing depression and losing their confidence increase. It has been demonstrated that strength training increases general self-efficacy and can help lower the risk of depression.

- **Lowers the risk of chronic disease:** Strength training is advised for most older people to help minimize the symptoms of the following chronic conditions: arthritis, osteoporosis, diabetes, obesity, back pain, and depression.

RECOMMENDED STRENGTH TRAINING EXERCISES FOR RUNNERS OVER 50

Seniors should use unilateral exercises to enhance balance, repair muscular imbalances and functional deficits, and complex, multi-joint exercises to increase strength.

Strengthening the back and core is crucial to improve posture, balance, stability, breathing mechanics, and movement effectiveness.

Claiming that there is a definite list of the most effective strength training exercises for people over 50 would be naive. The optimal exercises for you will vary depending on your needs, goals, and physical limits.

Following that, here are some of our preferred senior strength training exercises:

1. Forearm Plank

- Place your forearms flat on the floor as you start by lying down, ensuring your elbows are directly beneath your shoulders.

- Squeeze your abdominal muscles to lift your body off the floor while maintaining a straight line from your head to your feet and your forearms on the ground. Don't allow your hips to rise or fall; instead, keep your abs tight. Instead of 12 reps, hold for 30 seconds. Put your knees on the floor if it affects your low back or gets too challenging.

Targets: core, shoulders

2. Modified Pushup

- Kneel on a mat with your hands below your shoulders and your knees behind your hips to create a long, inclined back.

- To lower the chest toward the floor, tuck your toes beneath, contract your abs, and bend your elbows. Keep your eyes forward to your fingertips to maintain a long neck.

- Raise your chest to the starting position.

Targets: core, arm, and shoulders

3. Basic Squat

- Place your feet hip-distance apart while standing tall. Your toes, knees, and hips ought to be pointed forward. (To make it harder, hold dumbbells in your hands.)

- Bend your knees and extend your buttocks rearward as if you were going to recline back onto a chair. Keep your weight on your heels and your knees behind your toes. Rise and repeat.

Targets: hamstrings, quads, and glutes

4. Stability Ball Chest Fly

- While maintaining a tabletop position with the rest of your body, place your head and shoulder blades on top of the stability ball while holding a set of dumbbells near your chest. Hip distance should separate the feet.

- With the palms facing in, raise the dumbbells straight over the chest.

- When your elbows are approximately chest level, slowly lower your arms out to the side while maintaining a tiny bend in your elbow.

- Squeeze your chest and reunite your hands at the top.

Targets: core, glutes, back, and chest

5. Stability Ball Triceps Kick Back

- With your legs extended to the floor behind you, place your chest on the ball while holding dumbbells in each hand. Keep your head and spine in alignment. Without a ball, you can also stand with your feet staggered from front to rear and your body tilted forward.

- To start, raise your elbow to a 90-degree angle.

- Press the dumbbells back to stretch your arms and squeeze your triceps.

- Release dumbbells to their initial position.

Target: Triceps and the core

6. Shoulder Overhead Press

- Place your feet hip-distance apart to begin. Dumbbells should be held at the side of the head; arms should form a goalpost, and abdominal muscles should be tight.

- Gently raise the dumbbells until your arms are straight. Return with control gradually to the starting position. If you'd like, you may also carry out this exercise while sitting in a chair or standing on a stability ball.

Targets: the back, biceps, and shoulders

7. Stability Ball Overhead Pull

- With your head and shoulder blades on top of the ball and your body in a tabletop position, hold a pair of dumbbells near your chest while performing this exercise. Hip distance should separate the feet.

- With the palms facing in, raise the dumbbells straight over the chest.

- Slowly lower your arms behind your head while maintaining a tiny bend in your elbows.

- Pull the arms back to the starting position over the chest while contracting your lats.

Target: the back and the core

8. Stability Ball Side Leg Lift

- Kneel and place the ball by your right side.

- Wrap your right arm around the ball while allowing your right side to slant slightly toward it.

- Extend left leg long to the side. On the floor, the right leg should remain bent.

- Lift and lower your left leg eight to twelve times slowly, then switch sides.

Target: The legs and the core

9. Single Leg Hamstring Bridge

- Lie on your back and ensure your feet are flat on the ground and your knees bent at hip distance.

- Squeeze your glutes and raise your hips into a bridge position. Repeat on the opposite side, lowering and raising the hips for 8–12 reps.

Targets: Quads, glutes, and hamstrings

10. Bird Dog

- Kneel on the mat on all fours.

- Reach out with one arm and extend the opposite leg far behind you.

- Perform 8–12 reps before switching sides.

Targets: back and core

INCORPORATING STRENGTH TRAINING INTO YOUR ROUTINE

Can you run and build strength at the same time? The answer is yes if that's what you want to know. It's encouraged.

But occasionally, the real question is: Is it possible to build muscle while losing weight? This has a more complex solution.

You should be in a calorie surplus if you want to build more muscle mass. You'll likely eat more calories than usual to consume enough protein for your body to develop larger muscles. Essentially, this is the bulking phase of the bulk and cut you often hear about.

You must have a calorie deficit to lose weight. It is impossible to be in a calorie surplus and a calorie deficit simultaneously. Because of this, it can be difficult to simultaneously gain muscle and reduce weight, considering running burns much fewer calories.

It is difficult to gain more muscle, train frequently, run, offset calorie expenditure, and consume enough protein simultaneously. Focusing on one is preferable because of this.

Running and strength training complement each other very effectively in addition to physically developing bigger muscles. Strength training is always good and can be done successfully with a running regimen to increase strength and endurance. You'll succeed and feel better overall if you improve these many forms of fitness.

Fitting it all in

The challenge of incorporating two different fitness training modalities into your program is typically doing so without feeling as though your progress is being slowed somehow.

You are always in control of how often you train. There is no golden rule. What matters is what your goals are.

If improving your running is your primary goal, you should set a weekly goal of 2-3 runs and 1-2 strength training sessions. But with this split, you can improve your running while getting help from strength training. Consider where you are now and where you want to be while determining frequency.

Aim for three to four resistance exercises and one to two runs each week if building strength is your primary objective.

You can perform strength training and run on the same day if you don't want to exercise every day of the week. One amazingly well-rounded workout consists of a 40-minute upper body workout and a 20-minute treadmill run.

Understanding and observing your rest days will significantly influence your routine.

Days for rest and recovery

Rest and recovery as just as crucial as the action itself. Your body requires downtime to unwind, heal, and recharge. Rest days are essential for strength training. Your muscles will suffer exercise-induced injury from the work you do in the gym, which they must recover from to grow bigger and stronger. Your training programs need to take this into account. Refrain from repeatedly exercising the same muscle groups. To give different muscle groups ample time to heal, split your workouts.

Running doesn't cause the same muscular damage as other sports, but it doesn't mean you shouldn't rest. Your joints and muscles will be at risk of overuse because this is a repetitive activity if you don't take a rest. Additionally, new runners must exercise caution to avoid doing too much too soon. If not, you may be sure you will feel it the following day. The best way to move forward is "gradually."

Be sure to pay attention to your body's signals. It does a pretty decent job of communicating what it wants and needs.

Get the correct macronutrients.

Be sure to eat enough of the right foods to fuel your body and aid your recovery after your workout.

Ensure you consume enough carbohydrates if your runs leave you feeling lethargic and weak. When you run, your body uses carbohydrates as its primary energy source; if you don't have enough, it will have to work harder to convert to other sources, resulting in decreased performance. This is particularly valid for lengthier routes that take more than 90 minutes.

It's okay if you like to run before breakfast in the morning. But if you feel too weak to make it through, you might want to reconsider your refueling plan. Immediately after your run, try to eat some carbohydrates to replace your energy. A banana is a reliable signal.

You must consume enough protein to ensure your muscles regenerate and heal. Your body needs protein for the majority of its daily tasks. The remainder is then required to heal muscle damage brought on by exercise. You should focus on protein if you plan to lift weights.

The daily need for protein for the typical sedentary adult is 0.8g per kg of body weight. Exercise will cause this to rise to about 1.2g. Elite athletes require more than 2.0g. Make sure you're getting plenty wherever you are.

Flexibility and stretching

Please pay attention to these two points. You will benefit from mobility exercises and stretching in all facets of fitness. However, they presumably receive the least focus.

Set aside time to care for your muscles. Not when you have DOMs; Every day. After a workout or earlier if you choose.

Maintaining a sufficient range of motion requires mobility work, which also includes keeping your muscles and joints healthy so you can perform all your exercises with proper form.

Your flexibility is improved by stretching. It won't relieve tightness right away. Stretch after each session to ensure high flexibility after repetitive exercises like running. In doing so, you'll eventually contribute to a decrease in muscular tension. Pun intended.

Put interval training in

Running and resistance training both benefit from interval training. It's a time-tested method for simultaneously increasing muscular endurance, anaerobic fitness, and aerobic fitness.

Running intervals may consist of quick bursts at a faster pace followed by long bouts at a slower pace. You will improve your ability to work more quickly and intensely as a result.

Resistance training intervals may comprise pre-planned work and recovery periods of various low-resistance activities. The most significant thing to remember is that lower weights are used instead of heavier ones. It would be best to concentrate on lifting heavier weights for fewer reps with long breaks in between for strength training. It's not an excellent approach to strength train, but it can help you increase your muscle endurance.

CHAPTER 6

NUTRITION FOR RUNNING INJURY PREVENTION

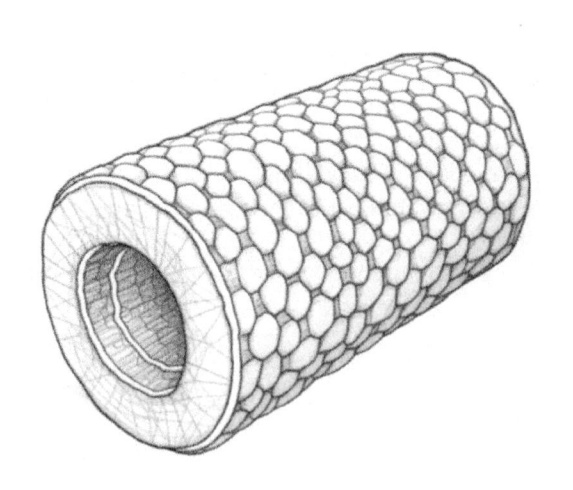

CHAPTER SIX

NUTRITION FOR RUNNING INJURY PREVENTION

Do you have any food you used to avoid as a kid but now consume regularly? As we age, our view of what goes into our body's changes, and we often develop a new respect for it. Perhaps this is because as we age, we become more conscious of the possibility of inheriting chronic diseases like diabetes and heart disease. Could it be that the dreaded "slow metabolism" is to blame?

It's difficult to deny that we, as competitive athletes, want to set no boundaries, despite age-related health concerns. Colleen De Rueck and Joan Samuelson are my favorite female runners. These athletes give masters competition new life. They serve as an encouraging example of what people of all ages are capable of.

If master's runner decides to keep fueling their competitive desire over the years, their training may need to change. Do they also need to change their diet?

OVERVIEW OF THE IMPORTANCE OF PROPER NUTRITION FOR RUNNERS

The success of a half or full marathon depends as much on your food and nutrition as it does on your physical preparation. Ensuring the body has adequate fuel to operate and recover is crucial. Your body will be prepared for race day by including healthy eating habits in your training. The following foods are the ones you need to eat most:

Carbohydrates

The body's primary energy for running is glycogen, which the body uses to store carbohydrates. You should consume 65 percent of your daily calories from carbohydrates, preferably complex carbohydrates. It is advised that runners increase their daily caloric intake by 100 calories for every mile they run while training.

Good examples of complex carbohydrates include the following: raisins, cereal, apples, syrup, bagels, brown rice, apples, corn, carrots, root vegetables, yams, potatoes, beans, wheat bread, peas, bananas, spaghetti, macaroni, and cereal.

Protein

You should consume daily amounts of 0.5 to 0.7 grams per pound of body weight. Also, it is advised that 10% of a runner's diet should consist of protein. This will facilitate the healing of muscular tissue.

Examples of good sources of protein include chicken, lean beef, fish, beans, eggs, green peas, yogurt, cheese, almonds, cottage cheese, peanut butter, tofu, and soy products.

Fats

When training, unsaturated fats should comprise 20–25 percent of your daily calories. Examples of unsaturated fats include Avocado, salmon, almonds, nut butter, seeds, and vegetable oil.

Vitamins

A daily multivitamin is advised to ensure your body has enough minerals. Moreover, runners require a lot of calcium and iron; therefore, look for foods high in these nutrients.

RECOMMENDED NUTRIENT-DENSE FOODS FOR RUNNERS

You need to have more than just solid training to run well. You should also consider what you put into your body to increase your speed and performance. Eating the correct nutrients at the proper time improves your ability to run efficiently. Also, you will lower your chance of illness and injury.

1. Bananas

A banana is an excellent choice if you need a high-carb energy boost before your afternoon run. Moreover, this fruit has a good amount of potassium (about 400 mg). This is crucial for long runs in hot weather when you are more prone to s lot and lose critical minerals. Potassium makes up for this loss and decreases your blood pressure simultaneously, along with other minerals like salt, magnesium, and chloride.

2. Oats

Oatmeal is the ideal breakfast option if you want to run after breakfast. It gives you a lot of carbs (approximately 25 g per serving) and is high in fiber.

A low glycemic index is another benefit of oats. This indicates that they gradually raise your blood sugar level, give you energy over a longer time, and prolong your sense of fullness. Did you also know that a healthy adult needs to acquire roughly 50% of their energy from carbohydrates?

3. Peanut Butter

We're discussing pure peanut butter without other ingredients like sugar, salt, or oil.

Vitamin E, the most potent antioxidant of all the vitamins, is reasonably present. While it is true that peanuts are high in fat (and therefore not low in calories), most of that fat comprises monounsaturated and polyunsaturated fatty acids. These may aid in lowering blood cholesterol levels.

Peanut butter is a crucial component of a runner's diet because it is high in protein and promotes muscular growth. Also, they are essential for boosting your immune system, accelerating your post-run recovery, and avoiding injuries. Try spreading peanut butter and banana slices on whole-grain bread; it's delicious! It is also tasty when combined with a few apple slices.

4. Broccoli

This leafy green vegetable is one of the most excellent foods for runners since it is rich in vitamin C. Do you know why? According to studies, vitamin C may prevent painful muscles after strenuous exercise. The nutrients calcium, folic acid, and vitamin K, which help to strengthen our bones, are also abundant in broccoli. We recommend pairing broccoli with tofu, fish, or lean meat.

5. Plain yogurt

The macronutrients, protein, and carbs are the ideal pairing in yogurt.

It has a value of almost 85%, indicating that a significant portion of the amino acids is necessary (which cannot be synthesized by the body and must be obtained through food). When consumed immediately following a run, it helps hasten your recuperation and safeguard your muscles. Also, the calcium in them helps to strengthen your bones. Yogurt also has the advantage of containing live lactic acid bacteria (probiotics). They promote healthy gut flora, which supports your immune system. Everyone should be aware of this, not only runners.

6. Dark chocolate

You are entitled to reward yourself occasionally for your dedication to running. Dark chocolate (at least 70% cacao) may reduce blood pressure and cholesterol levels.

Also, flavonols, which are secondary metabolites, aid in reducing inflammation.

7. Whole-grain pasta

It is not by chance that pasta parties are often held the night before marathons. These activities help you prepare mentally for the race the next day, and the high-carb lunch also fills up your glycogen reserves. You have all the energy you need to finish the marathon thanks to full glycogen stores.

Use whole-grain pasta and bread whenever possible because they contain more B vitamins (like bananas) and will keep you fuller longer. They are crucial for gaining muscle and can also increase your performance and endurance. For instance, enjoy your pasta with tuna and tomato sauce instead of the heartier carbonara sauce. Although it doesn't feel as heavy in your stomach, it is still calorie-dense.

8. Coffee

According to studies, a cup of coffee can improve your high-intensity interval training. Because of the caffeine in it, you may run farther and faster.

It's crucial to consume black coffee - devoid of milk and sugar. Contrary to popular belief, coffee doesn't cause dehydration in the body. Coffee does boost pee production, so you might need to use the restroom more often than usual, which is probably not a good idea during a marathon, now that you think about it.

9. Potatoes

Like bananas, potatoes are an excellent source of potassium and are a necessary part of every runner's diet.

Their calorie count is also important to note. For instance, compared to 100 g of rice, the famous vegetable has two-thirds fewer calories per 100 g. They create a nutritious and delectable recovery meal with lean chicken, fish, or fried eggs. Did you know that a single giant sweet potato can provide all your daily needs for vitamin A? This vitamin is an antioxidant that enhances vision, fortifies bone structure, and strengthens the immune system.

10. Beet

Did you know that beet can help with muscle discomfort relief? This vegetable is rich in secondary metabolites and antioxidants, strengthening the immune system and promoting good health in athletes.

Have you ever had a feta and walnut-topped red beet salad? It has a great flavor and is nutrient-rich.

11. Ginger

Ginger's potent chemical component, gingerol, gives it its fiery flavor. Research has indicated that consuming 2 grams of ground ginger, or 60 milligrams of ginger extract, one hour before working out will lessen muscular discomfort.

12. Eggs

Are eggs healthy? Their negative reputation is actually out of date.

Hen's eggs contain all the essential amino acids, numerous vitamins, and other vital nutrients. They help in the rehabilitation and growth of muscles. As a result, they are among the healthiest foods for runners, especially when consumed shortly after a run (ideally combined with a carbohydrate).

13. Flax Seeds

Flax seeds are an authentic superfood. You may add them to your smoothie, salad, or breakfast cereal.

Omega-3s reduce oxidative stress and inflammation, which is especially advantageous for athletes who train hard. They are especially valuable since they contain a lot of omega-3 fatty acids.

14. Legumes

Not just runners but everyone needs a healthy stomach. Fiber helps you maintain a healthy metabolism, normal digestion, and a robust immune system.

You should include high-fiber foods in your meal plan every day. Which are:

- Legumes
- Fruit and vegetables
- Seeds
- Whole grains and whole-grain products

15. Dried Fruit

The best part about dried fruit is that it is sweet and delicious, making it the ideal pre-run snack for runners. Examples of dried fruit include apricots, figs, and dates. They provide you with energy quickly because they are essential carbs. Moreover, dried fruit is a rich source of beneficial minerals such as magnesium and potassium.

HYDRATION TIPS FOR RUNNERS OVER 50

The health and performance of runners depend on maintaining hydration. Our body temperature is regulated by water, and it also flushes out waste, aids in supplying energy to our cells, and cushions our joints. Hydration is essential for maximizing performance, minimizing cramping and damage, and improving recovery.

Sweating serves to cool down our bodies. We produce 20 times more heat when we are moving than when we are at rest. The loss of water and electrolytes, such as salt and potassium, is a side effect of sweating. Dehydration can occur if we lose more fluid than two to three percent of our body weight (3 to 5 pounds for a 150-pound person). Dehydration can cause fatigue, headaches, cramps, and an elevated heart rate. Performance may be affected.

To stay hydrated, consider the following advice:

1. Recognize your sweating rate.

Before and after an hour-long or longer run, take your weight. 20–24 ounces of water should be consumed in place of each pound of body weight loss. Eat foods like a peanut butter and jelly sandwich that are high in carbohydrates and electrolytes while doing this. Carbs will replenish your muscles, and your body will use the electrolytes daily.

Your sweating rate is affected by numerous things. They include the outside temperature, how hard you run, your body type, how long you run, and your fitness level. For instance, trained runners tend to sweat more than less fit runners because their bodies are more adept at cooling themselves.

2. Drink regularly.

The easiest strategy to replace fluid losses is to consume water throughout the day rather than all at once.

- Drink water throughout the day

- Eat fruit. Fruit is a fantastic source of fiber, electrolytes, and hydration.

- The strongest indicator of hydration status is not simply being thirsty. Check to see that your pee is transparent to light yellow instead. Drink up if it's darker.

- Before consuming alcohol, hydrate. Alcohol can dehydrate you and cause your muscles to store carbohydrates insufficiently, resulting in decreased performance and a higher risk of injury.

3. Hydrate yourself before, during, and after a run.

Just as crucial as drinking during the rest of the day is before, during, and after exercise.

- Drink at least 16 ounces (2 cups) of water two hours before your run. Include a snack or meal with this.

- Six to eight ounces of water should be consumed around 15 minutes before a run.

- During a run lasting more than an hour, drink water frequently. Your sweat rate affects how much you perspire. Every 15 minutes, people who sweat more heavily might need 16 ounces of water. Together with water, you should also eat some carbs and replenish your electrolytes. Examples include gels for sports and dried fruit.

- Aim for at least 16 ounces of water with food after a run. Or, if you are aware of your sweat rate, replenish each pound lost with 20 to 24 ounces.

IMPORTANCE OF RECOVERY NUTRITION

The significance of recovery nutrition is influenced by the kind and extent of the just concluded exercise, the desired body composition, and individual preferences. Recovery nutrition aims to:

- Properly feed and hydrate the body
- Promote muscle development and repair
- Increase adaptability following a run
- Support immunological function.

It's crucial to practice a proactive recovery diet whether you do two or more training sessions in a single day or two sessions quickly after one another (e.g., an evening session followed by an early morning session the next day). Nonetheless, recovery nutrition is still necessary whether you train daily or a few times weekly. Still, you might be able to satisfy your nutrition goals with regular meals or snacks rather than consuming extra food.

THE ROLE OF ANTIOXIDANTS IN INJURY PREVENTION

You probably picture something good and something you've been urged to eat more of when you hear the word "antioxidants." How does an antioxidant affect your health and running, and what precisely is an antioxidant?

What are antioxidants? Where can we find them?

Antioxidants are natural or synthetic chemicals that can postpone or stop cell deterioration. The things we eat, like vegetables, fruits, chocolate, tea, and coffee, naturally contain many antioxidants. The antioxidant properties of vitamins C, E, beta-carotene, and selenium are likely familiar to you. Other substances, such as phytochemicals, like lycopene in tomatoes, anthocyanins in blueberries, and catechins in green tea, also have antioxidant characteristics. Antioxidants are also available as supplements.

The impact of antioxidants on our health

Antioxidants reduce or stop the harm that free radicals—also known as reactive oxygen species or oxidants—cause to our bodies and the environment. Free radicals are unstable because they have an unpaired electron, which gives them the potential to damage human cells and increase stress levels in the body. Free radicals constantly threaten us because of pollution, smoking, radiation, and exercise (yes, even exercise creates stress in the body). Free radicals have been related to various chronic diseases and can lead to inflammation in the body. By providing an extra electron, antioxidants work to neutralize these free radicals and ROS, making them more stable and less dangerous.

Although eating more antioxidants for improved health might seem obvious, that is only sometimes the case. In typical conditions, our body's antioxidant systems can control our stress. Yet, excessive amounts of exogenous antioxidants may render our body's natural antioxidant system ineffective. We, therefore, want to maintain a balance between oxidants and antioxidants.

What effect do antioxidants have on performance?

Antioxidants have been associated with improved performance and aerobic capacity during exercise. Acute antioxidant intake, such as vitamin E, may improve athletic performance by lowering oxidative stress markers and enhancing recovery. Nonetheless, because the presence of oxidants upregulates our body's antioxidant system, the ROS generated may provide some benefits in exercise and training adaptations. In other words, having some ROS in our bodies helps us build a more robust tolerance to handling it, leading to better performance and recovery, upregulated antioxidant defenses, and increased muscle growth.

CHAPTER 7

SLEEP AND INJURY PREVENTION

CHAPTER SEVEN

SLEEP AND INJURY PREVENTION

It is essential to get enough sleep, despite how alluring it may be to stay up late binge-watching television or to scroll through social media on your phone. A good night's sleep improves your performance the following day. Also, it helps in maintaining good health and a sharp mind. But why is it essential for runners?

According to science, sleep directly correlates with higher performance. Sleeping causes, the release of hormones that promote the synthesis of muscle proteins, mending the cellular damage caused by exercise. Your muscles sustain micro-damage to the tissues during exercise or a run, including muscle protein breakdown.

Sleep enables the body to repair itself. As a result, athletes often require more sleep than the average person. Most runners need 7-9 hours of sleep per night, while during intense training blocks, this number may be closer to 8-10. Little sleep can impact the immune system, raising your chance of getting sick. You'll feel it if you constantly get only a few hours of sleep; before you know it, your body will make you nap when you don't feel like it. Isn't it preferable to get enough rest and train rather than to neglect your sleep, become ill, and then be forced to take a break?

Let's examine how getting enough sleep might improve your running performance and make you stronger and quicker.

OVERVIEW OF THE IMPORTANCE OF SLEEP FOR RUNNERS

Runs, speedwork, and core and strength exercises are part of a runner's training regimen. Regularly getting a good night's sleep is another crucial component of effective training. Although runners and athletes sometimes ignore it, sleep is essential for recovery, muscular growth, and injury avoidance. One thing to first try when a runner has issues with injuries or endurance is getting 7-8 hours of sleep each night. The body cannot fully repair itself when a runner doesn't get enough sleep or stays up too late.

During a long run or intense speed workout, muscles are broken down and contain micro tears instead of growing during training sessions. Although the body can rebuild and strengthen the muscle to withstand further training sessions, this process primarily occurs while you sleep.

The body's temperature and pulse rate decrease as it enters the stage of relaxation while sleeping. The body releases growth hormones during the REM sleep period to repair muscle tissue. For optimum repair, the muscles are immobilized during this period.

A robust immune system also depends on getting enough sleep. When sleep is lacking, the body loses T-cells, crucial for activating and directing immune cells. Because of this, getting quality rest is equally important while we're sick.

REM sleep typically begins 90 minutes after falling asleep and lasts for two hours on average. The REM state might never be reached if a runner is too stressed or has trouble falling asleep. Long runs at high altitudes may influence sleep quality, particularly for ultrarunners. The resting heart rate is higher after lengthy, vigorous runs, which impacts the sleep cycle. After an Ultra race, the resting heart rate often takes a few days to return to normal. Rest and rehabilitation after a race are essential for this reason.

THE IMPACT OF SLEEP ON RECOVERY AND PERFORMANCE

There are many methods for preventing injuries during running, such as dynamic stretching, appropriate cross-training, and gradually increasing your distance. But here's a crucial strategy to think about getting a good night's sleep.

The Journal of Science and Medicine in Sport has released research that examined 95 endurance athletes, including runners, swimmers, cyclists, and triathletes. Researchers monitored sleep quality, training load, new injury episodes over a year, and complaints about cardiorespiratory problems, digestive troubles, and psychological struggles.

They discovered that people who reported getting less than seven hours of sleep each night had the highest rise in injuries. Injuries were more likely to occur for people who said psychological problems; however, the risk wasn't as significant as it was with the sleep relationship.

In contrast, there was no connection between increased training loads and new injuries for individuals reporting health concerns.

According to W. Chris Winter, M.D., owner of the Charlottesville Neurology and Sleep Medicine clinic and author of The Sleep Solution, this strengthens earlier studies that linked quality sleep to benefits in athletic performance. He routinely worked with sports teams and told Runner's World that more people are becoming aware of the importance of sleep for injury avoidance and efficient recovery.

Since adults primarily secrete growth hormones during deep sleep, he said, "it makes a lot of sense to see sleep as a tool for athletic performance." He added that this process is essential for protein synthesis, muscle recovery, immune system function, and modulation of your body's inflammatory response.

It makes sense that persistent sleep deprivation or a sleep disorder would harm an athlete, he added. They become sick more often and take longer to recover from injuries, which may reduce the time they can play their sport.

Another benefit, particularly for older women, comes from a recent sleep study published in the Journal of Bone and Mineral Research. According to the survey, including more than 11,000 postmenopausal women, those who slept five hours or less per night had lower bone density than those who slept seven hours or more.

Research revealed that sleep issues cause mood disturbances and increase general health complaints; even mood for athletes might be affected. This research was published in the journal Physical Therapy in Sports.

In conclusion, getting adequate sleep every night—around eight hours—is crucial for avoiding injuries, maintaining strong bones, and improving your mood for years to come.

STRATEGIES FOR IMPROVING SLEEP QUALITY

Below are five suggestions to help you become a champion sleeper and get the 8 to 10 hours per night that are advised:

1. Caffeine-free afternoon

You might have difficulty falling asleep and wake up more often than you should at night. Drinking too much coffee after noon may prevent you from falling asleep, even if it's fantastic for waking up in the morning and helping you stay productive. This will lower the quantity of our sleep and keep us from falling asleep deeply, which is necessary to wake up feeling rested and ready to take on the day.

2. Stop taking naps.

A nap during the day or late at night might make it harder to fall asleep when it's time to go to bed. A simple strategy to fall asleep faster and sleep better overall is to stop taking naps during the day and get to bed earlier.

The National Sleep Foundation advised keeping naps to no more than 20 minutes if you can't function without them. This should be fine with your typical sleep routine, leaving us feeling revived rather than sleepy. This is because, after a twenty-minute nap, we are not likely to awaken from a much deeper sleep than we may be after a thirty or forty-minute nap.

3. Limit exposure to blue light

Before going to bed, you should limit exposure to blue light. Blue light disrupts our circadian clock, which tricks our brain into believing it is daytime. This lowers the levels of hormones in our bodies, including melatonin, which promotes relaxation and sleep.

Try turning off all displays at least two hours before bed, putting your smartphone in night mode, and using blue-blocking glasses to decrease your exposure to blue light.

4. Have a schedule.

Lack of consistency in waking and sleeping hours is one of the more common causes of poor sleep. People with irregular sleep patterns often feel drowsy and exhausted and have more difficulty falling asleep. Our body's circadian rhythm operates on a loop and responds nicely to a regular routine.

Establish a daily wake-up and sleep time that is both realistic and consistent. Make sure to give yourself at least 8 to 10 hours of sleep every night, particularly if you're planning a long run, tempo run, or challenging interval workout.

5. Establish the ideal temperature

All of us have had sleep issues, particularly in the sweltering summertime. Finding and maintaining the ideal temperature (not too hot or chilly) is crucial to fall asleep quickly and sleeping soundly. Room temperature about 65 degrees Fahrenheit, or 20 degrees Celsius, is widely recommended. You can experiment with these and see what works best for you.

UNDERSTANDING THE EFFECTS OF SLEEP DEPRIVATION ON INJURY RISK

Imagine that you are about to compete in a significant race. You've already decided how to prepare for the race and how many miles you must run weekly. Like how you likely prepared your nutrition, you probably also planned your pre-race carbohydrate loading. You are also considering the running shoes you will put on to achieve your greatest results. What about your sleep, however? Like many runners, you might not have thought about the relationship between sleep and performance. But if runners want to perform at their best, this is still one of the most crucial training factors.

Impact of Sleep Deprivation on Running

Undoubtedly, life is busy, and people often need more sleep. This is unquestionably true for runners who want to log more miles. Not only can our training cut down on our sleep time, but exercise, in general, necessitates more sleep to get the optimum results. In light of this, you need to be aware of several running-related impacts of sleep deprivation.

- **Diet** - When we regularly lack sleep, our appetites change. Ghrelin, a hormone that increases hunger, is produced more often when we get too little sleep. Leptin, which alerts us when we're full, is likewise decreased by it. This can consequently result in overeating and weight gain. But obtaining enough sleep stops this from happening. In this way, if we regulate our sleep better, our weight and running performance may improve.

- **Metabolism** - Sleep deprivation interferes with the body's metabolism and impacts our hunger. Before a significant race, runners rely on their bodies' capacity to store carbs. As a result, we avoid "hitting the wall." Yet, lack of sleep makes the body less capable of doing this. As a result, running our best race may be more difficult, particularly if it's an endurance contest.

- **Injury Risk** - Sleep quality and running efficiency are very closely related. In addition to its natural restorative properties, sleep is crucial for mending damaged muscles and tissues. Human growth hormone, released during deep sleep, has been found to aid in this procedure. Yet, insufficient sleep inhibits the release of this hormone, which may impair our capacity to recover from a run. Injuries may result from this, in addition to tiredness and exhaustion.

- **Motivation** - Last but not least, getting too little sleep can make us less motivated to run. Good sleep promotes performance when running and boosts motivation. Yet, lack of sleep raises the likelihood that you'll have a dull, apathetic mood. As a result, you'll be less likely to follow your training schedule and accomplish your running goals.

THE ROLE OF SLEEP IN INJURY PREVENTION AND PERFORMANCE OPTIMIZATION

Are you getting adequate sleep? If you are active, getting too little sleep increases your risk of suffering a sports injury. Your body will suffer if you don't get regular, sound sleep. The benefits of sleep for athletes will be discussed here, along with some suggestions for getting a better night's sleep.

Your health and your body's capacity to regenerate depend on adequate sleep. Lack of sleep makes it difficult to perform at your best and increases your risk of injury.

Injury prevention is essential for athletes or anyone who often exercises because it can keep you from participating in your favorite physical activity while you recover. Many studies have revealed a link between decreased sleep and increased sports injuries. This makes sense because it is generally known that lack of sleep affects both motor and cognitive abilities, which are essential for athletic performance. On the other hand, increasing sleep time (towards 10 hours each night) can enhance athletic performance.

Sleep is also essential in the days following a strenuous workout. Even if you don't get injured during training, exercising causes numerous small tears in your muscle tissues, making recovery sleep crucial to promote muscle regeneration and allow your muscles to recover and get stronger. Also, sleep speeds up your body's physical healing from inflammation and replenishes your vitality.

Sleep deprivation affects performance.

Lack of sleep can make people feel drowsy and tired. The more sleep you get, the better your body can function. One study examined the effects of sleep on the performance of soldiers and workers in the transportation sector. This study shows that even one night of sleep deprivation can cause the body to react in a way comparable to intoxication. Participants in the study who slept for just 17 to 19 hours tested similar to having 0.05% blood alcohol concentration, and their response times were up to 50% slower.

Sleep Reduces Athletic Injury

Studies on lower amounts of sleep with adolescent athletes have linked poor sleep to greater injury rates, which this impact on performance may explain. Several studies have demonstrated a link between chronic sleep deprivation and an increased risk of musculoskeletal injuries (less than 8 hours per night for adolescents).

Sleep Affects the Immune System

The body cannot heal as rapidly when it is ill, which can result in downtime from activities. Your immune system's capacity to function is maintained by sleep. According to one study, research using a systems approach of neuroimmunology over the last 15 years has amassed surprisingly significant evidence that sleep boosts immunological defense, in agreement with the conventional belief that "sleep helps to heal."

Sleep Enhances Athletic Recovery

Sleep is necessary for your body to repair and renew bone, skin, and muscle tissue. Research demonstrated how sleep affected the body's regeneration processes and could aid healing. A study on how sleep affects injuries discovered that sleep deprivation significantly changed the molecular indicators of muscle regeneration.

Even the minor muscle rips caused by intensive training and exercise need time to heal to grow muscle. With sleep, the body will find it easier to keep up with exercise recovery periods.

CHAPTER 8

POSITIVE MENTAL STRENGTH AND INJURY PREVENTION

CHAPTER EIGHT

POSITIVE MENTAL STRENGTH AND INJURY PREVENTION

If you've ever run a long distance, you know running is much more complicated than it looks on the outside. Whether preparing for your first or next half marathon, remember to combine your strength and endurance training with mental preparation for running. Your mental strength will be put to the test.

Concentrate, relax, and keep your eyes fixed on the goal. Building mental power benefits many aspects of our lives, including at work, in the family, and during exercise. Fitness-related mental toughness is partly about adopting the appropriate mindset and staying calm and focused during workouts. Running long distances can truly benefit significantly from mental training.

OVERVIEW OF THE IMPORTANCE OF MINDSET AND MENTAL HEALTH

Mental strength is overcoming common negative emotions like tiredness, self-doubt, or discomfort to accomplish a specific goal.

Some contend that the ability to focus and mental strength are strongly associated, which is reasonable. It takes a tough athlete to concentrate on the task regardless of the environment, including the weather, the course's condition, other runners, or other factors affecting their performance. A mentally tough runner does not let these deterrents stop them from running.

Dan, an old friend, often comes to mind when considering this mental toughness. Dan has always been my antithesis in many respects, mainly because he is disciplined and laser-focused. We were both using treadmills to exercise at the gym one day when I realized he was missing his earbuds and wasn't even looking at the Screen. On the other hand, I was running while watching the screens and listening to music.

Not unexpectedly, Dan outperformed me significantly without actually keeping an eye on the time. Even now, I find it impossible to contemplate watching the seconds pass without going insane. But Dan can do that. Easy and happy. Dan's inherent resilience enables him to ignore all these other factors and give full attention to his run.

Running success depends heavily on mental toughness, especially for people over 50. Our bodies change as we age, affecting how physically capable we are. Yet, runners over 50 can keep running and accomplish their goals with mental toughness.

Most importantly, mental toughness enables runners to fight through difficulties and overcome barriers. Aches and pains, a loss of flexibility, and a decline in energy are all possible as we age. These elements can make it easy to quit running altogether. But with mental toughness, runners can concentrate on their goals and persevere in trying circumstances. They can have a positive outlook that enables them to view difficulties as chances for development and advancement rather than as insurmountable obstacles.

The capacity to control stress and worry is another advantage of mental toughness for runners over 50. Running can be an effective method for lowering stress and improving mental health. But for some people, especially as we age and our bodies become more prone to injury, it may also cause tension and concern. Runners can control these emotions and maintain a positive running relationship by developing mental toughness. Running can help you become more present and attentive, which will help you stay focused on the present moment rather than getting caught up in anxieties and fears about the future.

Mental toughness can help runners control their stress and anxiety and maintain their motivation and dedication to their goals. It can be easy to become complacent as we age and give up on our goals. Nonetheless, mental strength enables athletes to keep their goals in mind and challenge themselves. With mental strength, runners can develop a growth mentality that allows them to view failures as chances to learn and advance rather than justifications to give up.

Running can be a fantastic way to keep active and retain physical condition as we age. Also, having a strong mind can help runners become resilient and adaptable. Our bodies might not be able to manage as much intensity and volume as they once could as we become older. Running with mental toughness can help you adjust to these changes and find new challenges. Mentally strong runners may maintain their interest and drive to keep pursuing their passions, whether it is by cross-training, changing their running regimen, or setting a new goal.

Finally, for runners over 50, mental toughness can enhance general physical health and well-being. Running can be a fantastic way to keep active and retain physical condition as we age. Yet the advantages go beyond the purely physical ones. Running mentally strong athletes are likelier to adopt positive habits and behavior that promote well-being. This covers practices like controlling stress, getting enough sleep, and eating a balanced diet. Runners can adopt a holistic approach to their health and well-being that goes beyond just running by prioritizing mental toughness.

For runners over 50, mental toughness is a crucial element of success. Runners who practice mental toughness can overcome challenges, control stress and anxiety, maintain motivation, adjust to changes, and enhance their general health and well-being. Whether you're a seasoned runner or just getting started, mastering mental toughness is a crucial ability that may help you reach your goals and reap the many advantages of running.

UNDERSTANDING THE IMPACT OF STRESS ON INJURY

Stress is the mechanism through which the body and brain react to the demands or challenges of a circumstance, which can range from pressures at school or job to dealing with trauma or life upheavals. When faced with such obstacles and circumstances, the body typically responds by being stressed out to modify and adapt. Your body responds to stress by generating several physiological reactions, which are to blame for the symptoms of stress you encounter.

You might have a solid training schedule, a sensible eating plan, and the drive to finish your next run strong. Even while all of these things are highly important, it's also crucial that you pay attention to your stress levels. Despite your planning, a single stressor could still derail your training. The stress brought on by such occurrences can have an adverse effect on how well you run, whether you are going through a difficult time in your personal life or at work.

How does your body respond to stress?

Although it may not be immediately apparent, stress impacts several bodily systems, including the endocrine, cardiovascular, and musculoskeletal systems, to mention a few. As was previously said, being under stress sets off several physiological processes that aid in assessing the situation and providing a bodily response to the stressor.

A sequence of physiological responses is triggered when the body senses a demand or a threat, preparing you to respond to the stressor. Stress chemicals like cortisol and adrenaline are released. Your heart rate, blood pressure, and energy level all rise when you are under the effects of adrenaline. Blood sugar levels rise, and glucose utilization is enhanced by cortisol. Your focus improves, your senses grow more acute, your reaction time quickens, and you gain the strength to confront or escape the threat.

Unfortunately, stress is a regular part of every person's daily existence. Your body may experience several health problems due to the steady increase in stress. Chronic stress or stress that persists over time disrupts the body's functions and can make you feel constantly overburdened, which makes you physically and mentally exhausted.

How does long-term stress impact your ability to run?

These are a few ways that persistent stress can affect your ability to run:

1. Recovery-related effects

Running puts the body through stress, similarly to any other exercise. Your body deteriorates with each exercise session, resulting in tissue damage. Recovering from these injuries is crucial since it enables your body to better withstand the stress of running and get stronger. You can do this to come back week after week to enhance your performance. Many substances, including cytokines, macrophages, growth factors, and hormones like cortisol, work together to trigger the inflammatory response needed to heal the damage brought on by exercise. When combined with its other effects, such as disrupted sleep patterns, stress can influence the amounts of these chemicals and hormones in the body, which may delay recovery.

Researchers from the Yale Stress Center and the University of Texas examined the impact of psychological stress on post-exercise muscle strength recovery in a study published in Medicine and Science in Sports and Exercise. They concluded that stress has a detrimental effect on post-exercise recovery, showing that people experiencing high-stress levels often recover more slowly than those who do not experience chronic stress.

2. The musculoskeletal system is impacted.

The musculoskeletal system may be impacted by stress. Cortisol in excess might cause a decrease in bone density. Moreover, it can cause the muscles to stiffen up, which is thought to be the body's response to stress to defend itself from harm. Your gait can be impacted by stiff muscles while running, resulting in poor form. Moreover, strained muscles could make it difficult to stand on solid ground.

Once the stress subsides, the muscles can begin to relax. But persistent stress can cause muscles to tense for extended periods activating the body's other stress-related systems and setting off stress-related health issues.

3. Impacts on athletic performance

Unfavorable/tragic life events or significant life changes that are seen negatively are believed to affect a person's psychosocial stress and recovery. A study examined the effect of negative life experiences on runners' abilities. The findings demonstrated that significant life events might negatively impact how people experience stress. Such occurrences may also affect their ability to recuperate in the week immediately following and the week the bad life event happened.

Three weeks after the bad life experience, they also indicated a decline in the running economy, demonstrating a relationship between stress and running performance. The brain's stress reaction may be to blame for the decline in the running economy after a traumatic life event.

The Rate of Perceived Exhaustion (RPE) scale, which has a scale from 1 to 10, is a subjective instrument often used to evaluate the intensity of your workout, its ease or difficulty, or how emotionally and physically draining it is. This is a standard tool used by runners to gauge the difficulty of their runs.

A study involving 20 runners showed that cognitive tiredness reduced their running performance as measured by slower finish times. This was due to higher RPE, which raised the impression of effort. Due to weariness, the respondents felt they had to exert more effort during their runs, which may have caused them to slow down to finish the distance. Additionally, there were no appreciable differences in physiological parameters like blood lactate levels and heart rate between the control group and the fatigued runners, indicating that even though all the subjects put an equal amount of effort into their running, cognitive fatigue caused the tired runners to perform worse.

4. Impacts on exercise

You may feel unmotivated, which could affect your training due to common stress effects like mood swings, changes in sleep and food patterns, and mood fluctuations.

Your capacity for decision-making may be impacted. Due to ongoing stress, you may become mentally exhausted, distracted, and less attentive. Being preoccupied can make it harder to notice when your body gives you symptoms. This may substantially impact your training. For instance, if you ignore the signs of overtraining, you could overtrain, which is a common reason for running injuries. Also, the effects of stress on your mental health can affect the results of your rehabilitation after an injury or illness.

MINDFULNESS AND MEDITATION TECHNIQUES FOR RUNNERS

Running meditation may be something you've previously tried if you've ever experienced a state of profound serenity and connectedness to the present moment while exercising.

Running meditation is exactly what it sounds like—meditation combined with exercise.

You might think meditation consists of sitting cross-legged, keeping your eyes closed, and remaining silent. Meditation, often performed in a calm environment free of distractions, can be about this.

Running can provide you with the opportunity to practice moving meditation. Running's rhythmic nature could allow you to put your troubles aside, calm your thoughts, and fully engage in the moment.

You can gain various advantages from running meditation. Also, there are particular ways to execute it to maximize its benefits.

What is running meditation?

Running meditation is a meditation in motion. While you exercise, it's essential to establish a connection with your body, calm your mind, and allow yourself to truly live in the moment.

If you lead a stressful life and feel you don't have the time to sit and contemplate your thoughts each morning, running meditation can be a perfect choice for you.

You can try to concentrate on your breathing and the feelings in your body while running rather than stressing about a project at work or other items on your to-do list.

The advantages of mixing meditation with exercise have been the subject of years of research. Meditation while engaging in physical activity will help you in:

- Lowering stress and anxiety
- Increasing pain tolerance
- Improving performance and flow state
- Improving sleep
- Lowering the risk of injuries
- Elevating mood and general well-being.

Everyone, from casual runners to professional athletes, can gain from incorporating meditation into their daily routines.

Running meditation may be highly beneficial if you struggle with any of the following conditions.

- Anxiety
- Intrusive thoughts
- Depression

Running and meditation are both excellent for controlling the symptoms of depression, but they work even better together.

The way the brain reacts to stressful events is changed by meditation. It reduces your reactivity and improves your ability to restrain unpleasant or unwanted feelings and ideas.

But it's crucial to remember that not everyone will benefit from running meditation. Concentrating on your body and thoughts may be challenging without endangering your safety. For instance, you should keep your eyes and ears open if you love running on busy streets.

To determine if mindful running suits you, you should also talk to your healthcare team about it.

Mindfulness vs. meditation

Meditation means focusing your concentration and awareness on achieving a peaceful and transparent state of mind. There are various meditation practices. One of them is mindfulness meditation.

Being mindful implies paying attention to the present moment. You can achieve this by concentrating on your breathing and the sensations in your body, mind, and emotions.

Running meditation is a type of mindfulness exercise.

HOW DO YOU MEDITATE WHILE RUNNING?

If you wish to run and meditate, take into account these suggestions:

1. Pay attention to your breathing

It's often advised to focus on breathing as the first stage in many meditation techniques. It can be a grounding force to quiet your thoughts and relax your mind.

You can start your running routine by taking a few deep breaths through your nose while relaxing your diaphragm and slowly exhaling. You can observe your breathing while you run more quickly rather than attempting to regulate it.

Start slowly and pick up the pace gradually while you pay attention to how your body adjusts to the increase in speed.

2. Making a resolution

Why do you run as you meditate? Establishing your goal and creating a statement to keep you focused is beneficial.

During running, if your thoughts stray, you can repeat the statement to help you get them back on track.

This might be a positive affirmation, a fantastic method to de-stress and unwind. You could use the phrase "I am fully involved with the present moment" as an example.

3. Eliminating earbuds

Running is fun when listening to music or a podcast. Yet, if you're trying to meditate, it could be annoying.

If you wear headphones, think about listening to or not using white or natural noises. Try various activities to see what keeps your mind clearer and what works best.

4. Leaving the house

When running on a treadmill, connecting with the present moment can be more difficult. And meditation might benefit from some fresh air.

Since you'll be meditating, picking a location free from hazards and traffic is crucial. Although paying attention to your body may make you less aware of your surroundings, the idea is not to shut out your environment.

Paying attention to your body and taking any pain seriously is also crucial. An injury could result from this.

3 TECHNIQUES FOR MINDFUL RUNNING

1. Becoming aware of your body

As you run, try to take a complete inventory of your body. When you do this, think about keeping a journal of any feelings.

Consider paying attention to how the air feels as it enters your nose or how warm it feels as it leaves your mouth. You can concentrate on the sensation of the breeze on your face or how the ground feels beneath your feet as you move. You should pay attention to the sweat drop ready to fall from your forehead.

Try to give each observation and sensation at least a few minutes.

2. Trying to escape criticism

It's beneficial to get in the habit of simply noticing your ideas as they come to you. This entails permitting thoughts to arise but then letting them go.

I must breathe more slowly. Try to focus on your breath or body without judging or categorizing it. Instead of saying, "I'm not breathing correctly," you may say, "I'm breathing quickly and shallowly."

3. Practicing gratitude

Running meditation has advantages that can be enhanced by giving thanks.

Try to be thankful for your freedom to move about, the sights and sounds you are experiencing, or the fact that you are taking care of yourself.

STRATEGIES FOR OVERCOMING MENTAL BLOCKS AND NEGATIVE THOUGHTS

Running is physically demanding because as you pound the pavement, your muscles deteriorate, and your joints suffer. Overcoming these obstacles can help you complete the race without losing your calm. Running the kilometers becomes much more challenging when your brain is not in the game, whether a 26.2-mile marathon or a 1-mile run around the neighborhood. A simple run, however, will become a hateful dash due to the mental challenge.

1. Get rid of your negative thoughts.

Spending the entire race worried about money or thinking back on a previous dispute will make your thoughts foggy and make you feel bad. Instead, try to quiet your mind and focus exclusively on the beauty of your surroundings, the clean scent of the grass, and how powerful your body feels.

2. Stop talking negatively to yourself as well.

Quit telling yourself that you won't be able to complete the run, that you are too exhausted, or that your body is in too much agony. Keep your inner dialogue optimistic by telling yourself how much you've accomplished and how well you're doing.

3. Create a mantra that breaks down barriers and repeat it to yourself as often as necessary.

Having a motto, you can go to when obstacles stymie you can be pretty helpful, whether it's a line from your favorite song, a beloved quotation, or something you make yourself. Repeat it aloud or in your brain if you need extra motivation.

4. Divide the distance into manageable chunks.

Divide a marathon into four five-mile halves rather than concentrating on the final 20 miles. Divide the remaining distance into landmarks if it is a lot shorter distance. Push until you reach the next street, or try to get to the pine tree in front of you. It is easier to overcome four small obstacles than one big one mentally.

5. Be eager to get to the finish line.

Choose a small reward for yourself before you even start the run, and keep your mind on it as you run. Consider the medal waiting for you at the finish line if you're running a marathon, or make plans to meet up with friends for a small meal after the run. If it's simply your daily run, perhaps you'll give yourself a little additional time to relax with a bubble bath or watch TV.

Adrian Ward

CHAPTER 9

MANAGING AND PREVENTING RUNNING INJURIES

CHAPTER NINE

MANAGING AND PREVENTING RUNNING INJURIES

A running-related injury will occur in one out of every three recreational runners at some point in their lives. Around 3 out of every four injuries sustained during running involve the lower leg. The foot, ankle, knee, and shin are common sites. Back and groin injuries are also common in runners.

Running is a wonderful sport that is easy, cheap, and thrilling. It has a lot of positive aspects, and it's unquestionably beneficial to both physical and mental health. Running, however, can be a cruel sport in terms of wear and tear due to the impact of each step, and injuries are common.

One strategy to deal with this is to respond to an injury as soon as it occurs. Yet, a more constructive attitude entails embracing the possibility of injuries and proactively managing and preventing them. It doesn't have to be difficult. Understanding why injuries occur and how to address them can be made easier by considering a few fundamental ideas.

Running does carry a risk of injury, but most injuries can be avoided by adhering to a few basic rules, like warming up, dressing appropriately, and not pushing yourself too hard.

OVERVIEW OF COMMON TREATMENTS FOR RUNNING INJURIES

Running injuries can take many different forms, and there are many different ways to treat them. The sort of injury you've incurred, your age, and your general physical condition all play a role in the proper course of treatment. Running injuries are often treatable without surgery. Conservative running injury treatments may include the following:

1. Using the RICE approach:

- Rest: Resting to allow the injury to recover properly
- Ice: Icing the affected area for brief periods
- Compression: Wrapping the damaged region to minimize swelling
- Elevating: Keeping the affected area will help to lessen pain and swelling.

2. Using over-the-counter pain relievers like aspirin or ibuprofen.

3. Keeping the wounded area immobile and preventing further harm by using a splint, cast, or walking aids (such as crutches).

4. Participating in physical treatment

5. Receiving cortisone injections to reduce pain and inflammation

6. Receiving joint injections to help degenerative disease-affected joints heal

Surgery might be required in extreme circumstances or for running injuries that don't improve with conventional therapies. The following surgical procedures are often used to treat injuries sustained while running:

- Hip arthroscopy
- ACL reconstruction surgery
- Open reduction and internal fixation (ORIF)
- Knee arthroscopy

THE IMPORTANCE OF EARLY INTERVENTION IN INJURY TREATMENT

Our bodies change as we age, and some of those changes might impact our physical capacities, including our ability to run. A reduction in muscular mass, flexibility, and cardiovascular fitness may occur in runners over 50, increasing their risk of injury. For runners over 50, early injury treatment is essential since it can limit future damage, hasten healing, and hasten return to running.

Overuse, improper technique, and underlying medical issues are just a few causes of injuries among runners over 50. Shin splints, plantar fasciitis, and knee pain are typical problems in this age bracket. Debilitating injuries like these could make it impossible for runners to keep up their fitness regimen. Early injury treatment, however, can lessen the severity of these wounds and keep them from becoming chronic.

For runners over 50, one of the critical advantages of early intervention in injury therapy is that it can stop future harm. Untreated injuries tend to worsen over time and cause more problems. For instance, if a runner over 50 has knee pain and keeps going without help, the pain could worsen, resulting in other situations like joint damage or arthritis. Runners can avoid these issues and protect their general joint health by seeking early intervention in injury therapy.

For runners over 50, early injury treatment can also hasten the healing process. Our bodies may take longer to recover from injuries as we age, and recovery times may be extended. Running athletes can, however, receive the care they require to heal properly and shorten recovery times by seeking therapy as soon as possible. This can help them resume running more quickly and stop them from losing ground toward their fitness goals.

Running injuries can be frightening and might make people unwilling to maintain their fitness regimen. Yet, runners can restore their confidence and feel more comfortable continuing their workout regimen by getting treatment and receiving the proper care as soon as possible. Early injury treatment for runners over 50 has the added benefit of assisting them in regaining their confidence when running. As exercise has been demonstrated to increase mood and reduce stress, this may benefit their mental and emotional health.

Aside from seeking early treatment for injuries, runners over 50 can take precautions to avoid getting hurt in the first place. To prevent injuries, you should warm up correctly before running, stretch frequently, wear the right shoes, and gradually increase the length and intensity of your runs. Paying attention to your body's needs and taking rest days when necessary is crucial.

Running has several advantages, including bettering one's physical and mental health, but only if injuries are prevented and treated as soon as they occur. Finally, for runners over 50, early injury treatment intervention is essential. It can stop further harm from happening, hasten the healing process, and assist runners in returning to running with confidence.

THE ROLE OF REHABILITATION AND PHYSICAL THERAPY IN INJURY PREVENTION

Your physical therapist must first understand the underlying cause of the injury before treating it. They will take as much time as necessary to understand your running goals, shoe preferences, and training routine. After that, a physical examination will be conducted to ascertain the following:

- The precise tissue that is injured

- The probable origin of the injury (training error; weakness; muscle imbalance; etc.)

- Any present habits that might be impeding the healing of the injury.

The examination will probably consist of running gait analysis, mobility testing using a hand-held dynamometer, and particular strength testing.

Running Gait Analysis

If necessary, your physical therapist will do a video gait analysis to record your gait pattern. This indicates movement patterns that contributed to your injury and places where you can increase performance quality and efficiency. Your therapist will be especially interested in identifying the following:

- How well (or poorly) do you currently tolerate running? This will assist in establishing a schedule and plan for returning to the desired running volume.

- Is there a feature of your chosen gait pattern that may be changed to help you handle running more easily?

Treatment Methods

Any deficiencies discovered during the initial test will be explained to you by your physical therapist. You and your physical therapist will explore treatment choices to address the relevant concerns with the most significant degree of effectiveness and the fewest number of appointments. Treatment typically includes the following:

- Training, cross-training, and relative rest education

- Progressive loading and strengthening exercises increase the load capacity of your tissues so they can endure the rigors of running.

- Retraining of gait. Your physical therapist may give you cues to change your running stride if advised to lessen discomfort, lessen the strain on injured tissue, increase running tolerance, and improve running economy and performance quality.

- Information on a home workout regimen. We at Endurance Physio place high importance on your recovery from therapy.

- Advice on how to start running again. How to resume running without reinjuring oneself is one of the trickiest aspects of rehabilitation. To return to the trails or roads as soon as possible without running into the danger of re-injury, your physical therapist will assist you in developing a strategy.

- Taping. Information on the best shoes and orthotics. Your physical therapist may employ taping procedures to enhance alignment, offload sore tissues, and lessen pain. You may also receive instructions on using foot orthotics or changing your shoes if necessary.

- Hands-on treatment. If necessary, you could get any of the following manual therapy treatments to help with pain alleviation, increased mobility, enhanced muscle activation, and muscle down-training (decreasing activation to overactive muscle groups):

    - Instrument Assisted Soft Tissue Mobilization and Soft Tissue Mobilization

    - Functional Dry Needling

    - Joint Mobilization

    - Muscle Energy Techniques (MET)

INCORPORATING INJURY-PREVENTION MEASURES INTO YOUR DAILY ROUTINE

First, what is injury prevention, and how should you avoid aches and pains? We've covered some excellent advice on preventing niggles from becoming injuries and lowering your risk of getting hurt in earlier chapters. In conclusion, injury prevention may involve the following:

- Making sure you get enough rest

- Fueling your workouts and recovering properly
- Following a well-structured training plan
- Paying attention to your body
- Following sensible warm-up and cool-down protocols before and after workouts
- Mobility work
- Rest and recovery.
- Strength and conditioning
- Physiotherapy/rehabilitation exercises
- Self-massage/myofascial release or deep tissue massage
- Regular check-ups with a physiotherapist

The list continues.

You can see that there are many different injury prevention methods, exercises, and best practices; trying to fit them all into a schedule that is already full can seem like an impossible effort. However, making little changes to your regular routine can enable you to incorporate some advantageous injury prevention practices without taking up a lot of additional time. The main emphasis of this section will be on strength and conditioning, as well as how to incorporate more into your day effortlessly. We won't concentrate on the specific exercises you should perform to avoid injury. Getting in touch with a certified personal trainer for a custom-structured strength and conditioning regimen is always advisable.

Including brief bursts of strength training is the best option if you don't have enough time to add regular stand-alone strength and conditioning sessions. little and frequently

We must develop new habits to incorporate more strength and fitness into our daily activities easily. For a new habit to stick, it must first satisfy the following requirements:

- It must be evident; otherwise, you'll forget to do it.
- It must be visually appealing, or you won't feel like starting.

- It must be easy because otherwise, it will appear impossible to complete.

- It must satisfy you; otherwise, you won't want to keep doing it.

Consider the following scenario: You want to incorporate more foam rolling into your everyday routine. How can we increase the likelihood that this new habit will last for the long run?

- Make it obvious – place your foam roller beside your bed or the TV. This way, you'll see it before you climb into bed or switch on the TV, making it less likely that you'll forget.

- Make it appealing by learning about the advantages of daily foam rolling; it might prevent injuries and even help you run faster!

- Keep it simple - Don't pressure yourself to "foam roll every day for 30 minutes"; habits need to be feasible, start small, and you'll be far more likely to stick with it. Develop the habit of foam rolling for 5 minutes each day.

- Make it satisfying. If you enjoy the discomfort, foam rolling alone may be enjoyable. Some could require a stronger perk. Complement it with a treat, ideally a healthy one. If I foam roll each day this week, I might reward myself with a weekend dinner out.

According to studies, scheduling where and when to conduct a new habit enhances the likelihood that it will stick. To take advantage of this feature, we employ a technique known as "habit stacking," in which they link behaviors and "stack" a new habit on top of an existing one.

Let's keep using the foam rolling illustration.

"I shall foam roll for five minutes before turning out the lights downstairs and going to bed."

We advise layering several habits on top of one another; however, we recommend building this up gradually. Keep in mind to keep it simple and appealing.

For instance, "I will foam roll for 5 minutes before turning off the lights downstairs on my way to bed, then put the foam roller back next to the TV and spend 1 minute stretching my calves on the stairs before walking upstairs to bed."

Above is a simple illustration of new behavior that can prevent injuries.

You will soon discover that you are carrying out the new habit without thinking about it. This technique can be applied to any technique you choose to prevent injuries, such as performing:

- Ten single-leg squats while brushing my teeth
- 15 glute bridges before putting on my running shoes
- 2 minutes of hip flexor stretching before taking off my running shoes
- Holding a 1-minute plank while waiting for the kettle to boil for my morning coffee.

Being patient is crucial. Transitions take time. These behaviors are tidbits of self-improvement that are little yet crucial. Even while these brief periods of activity may seem insignificant, they add up to have noticeable results over time. Consistency over an extended period is necessary for accurate fitness adaptation to occur. Daily bursts of strength and conditioning training can often produce better benefits than the irregular gym visits you hardly ever find time for in your busy schedule. Even though it may seem like nothing is happening, and you may think that practicing these exercises is a waste of time, maybe by this time next year, you can look back and will be able to say, "I haven't been injured over the year!"

Of course, the strategies offered here are helpful for more than just building strength and avoiding injuries. They provide a simple method for incorporating a variety of new, constructive behaviors into your life, such as making an effort to call a friend, engaging in daily meditation, or including that much-needed mobility work.

CHAPTER 10

STAYING MOTIVATED AND MAKING RUNNING A LIFESTYLE

CHAPTER TEN

STAYING MOTIVATED AND MAKING RUNNING A LIFESTYLE

It could be challenging to stand up and go for a run. Yet most of the time, getting up and doing it will make you feel better about yourself.

Consider the factors that led to your decision to run in the first place. You'll be more likely to find the drive to engage in an activity you genuinely want to undertake if you ask yourself if you enjoy running.

It's easy to find reasons to put off doing something, but the challenge is to provide justifications for doing it instead.

Action usually comes after motivation. So, gather your courage and start moving. After running, you'll feel better and be glad you stuck to your regimen.

Let's look at some advice that will inspire you to commit to your running schedule and amp up your game.

OVERVIEW OF THE IMPORTANCE OF STAYING MOTIVATED

Running is a well-liked exercise that has many positive effects on physical and mental health. Yet to succeed, it takes a lot of work and commitment, just like with any other exercise. It's essential to maintain motivation when running to reach one's goals. This is because motivation is crucial to their performance, whether a runner is running for fitness benefits or competitive reasons. In this chapter, we'll talk about how vital it is for runners to maintain motivation.

1. Motivation helps in goal-setting and achievement for runners.

A motivated runner is more likely to set and strive toward attainable goals. A runner needs goals because they give them direction and purpose. It helps them in figuring out their goals and strategies for achieving them. Without motivation, a runner may find it difficult to create goals and, even if they do, may lack the enthusiasm to pursue them.

2. Motivation helps in overcoming runners' challenges.

Running can be difficult, particularly for beginners. A runner could have moments of discouragement or encounter challenges like an injury or a lack of time. Running enthusiasts can overcome these challenges and continue because of their motivation. When motivated, the runner is more likely to discover answers to their issues and keep up their training.

3. Motivating oneself keeps runners consistent.

When it comes to running, consistency is essential. Regular running is necessary to increase fitness levels and accomplish goals. Consistency can be difficult to maintain, though, especially when life interferes. Motivation helps in keeping runners on track and consistent in their training. Motivated runners are more likely to stick to their training schedule and log frequent runs even when it's difficult.

4. Motivation helps in performance improvement for runners.

Since running is a sport that requires competition, many runners work to raise their standards. Since it provides them the drive and determination to exercise harder and push themselves to their limits, motivation is crucial for runners who wish to enhance their performance. Runners may find it challenging to increase their performance without motivation, and they may not be able to reach their maximum potential.

5. Motivation makes exercise enjoyable for runners.

Although it should be fun, running can occasionally be challenging. The motivated runner is more likely to find their training enjoyable. Running with motivation makes it easier to enjoy the journey and the process of reaching goals.

Maintaining motivation is essential for runners who want to accomplish their goals and enhance their performance. Setting and achieving goals, overcoming challenges, maintaining consistency, improving performance, and enjoying training are all made possible by motivation. Finding motivational tools that work for you as a runner is essential, whether creating attainable goals, finding a running companion, or rewarding yourself when you hit certain milestones. With running, anything is possible with the correct motivation.

SETTING REALISTIC AND ACHIEVABLE GOALS

Take a moment to visualize yourself winning a difficult race. Isn't it satisfying to see your smile, hear the crowd's applause, and realize that you have accomplished something extraordinary? Primary running goals, like finishing a race or covering a certain distance, are incredibly satisfying, but they typically don't happen without thoughtful goal-setting.

Continue reading to learn how to set and meet your running goals. There are only a couple more checkpoints to clear before you reach the finish line.

Why Setting Goals Is Vital for Runners

Setting running goals can help you divide your race, distance, or pace into more achievable segments, just like with any other eyes-on-the-prize target. You will likely feel like you've taken on only what you can handle if you set goals that increase gradually, which prevents you from being discouraged and giving up.

By setting clear goals, you can better understand what you want to accomplish from your running exercises. Here are some questions to consider:

- Are you preparing for a race?
- What speed would you prefer to maintain?
- How far do you wish you could run before being out of breath?
- How often would you like to run?

Consider jotting down and sharing your personal goals with a friend as you reflect on them. Those who shared weekly goal updates with a friend were twice as likely to achieve their goals than those who kept their goals to themselves.

Types of Running Goals

Each runner has a different motivation for lacing up. With all the advantages of running, your desired results could not be the same as those of another person.

Some possible running goals include:

- Running a certain distance, like one mile, five, or ten miles.
- Achieving health goals like weight loss, lowering blood pressure, or better blood sugar control.
- Meeting friends through a local running club.
- Signing up for and finishing a fun run or competitive race.
- Stress reduction or improving mental health

How to Establish Realistic Goals

The acronym SMART, which stands for Specific, Measurable, Attainable, Realistic, and Time-bound, is often helpful when defining goals. This simple mnemonic, which management consultants created in the early 1980s, has assisted numerous individuals in achieving their goals.

Making your goals more **specific** helps you focus so that you are more aware of what you are aiming towards. (Example: "I'd want to participate in my neighborhood's turkey run this November.") Similarly, keeping them **measurable** makes it obvious when you've achieved them—for example, after running a mile in 10 minutes.

Everyone's definition of "**attainable**" is different. Consider what your body is capable of before choosing a goal that might not represent the next letter: R for **realistic**. Finally, setting **time-bound** deadlines for your running goals will ensure you reach them as soon as possible.

How to Reach Your Running Goals

There are even more things you can do to adhere to your progress strategy in addition to setting SMART goals. To get you through to the end, try these five suggestions.

Be Committed

The beginning of a thousand kilometers is just one step, and the beginning of your running goal is just a simple commitment. Think about your SMART goal and make a written commitment to it. (Once more, telling a friend can help you stay accountable.) To keep your written goal top of mind, post it in a prominent location in your home.

Focus on Little Steps

You've probably heard that little things add up to huge things, and in this situation, both the metaphor and the literal are accurate. Earlier attention to smaller sub-goals in pursuing greater success increased people's motivation.

Try dividing your running goals into manageable steps as you progress toward them. Try a training plan where you gradually increase your mileage from 2 miles in week one to 2.5 miles in week two if you're preparing for a 10K. When race day finally arrives, switch your attention to how you'll complete the entire 6.2 miles.

Avoid Injuries

It makes sense to want to give it everything you've got when you have a goal in mind. But, overextending yourself and disregarding safety could result in injuries. Taking the proper precautions to avoid injury to achieve your running goals in good health is crucial.

Remember the best practices for avoiding mishaps and injuries, such as stretching before and after runs, using the proper footwear, being hydrated, and taking rest days. Moreover, if you run alone, make sure someone knows where you're going and when you'll be back.

Track Your Progress

It's easier to gauge your level of achievement if you keep track of your progress. Fortunately, you have a ton of tools at your disposal for tracking the distance, speed, heart rate, calories expended, and other aspects of your runs. Choose an app that works for you and use it to log each run. Seeing your development can give you the inspiration you require to keep going strong.

Reward Yourself

Rewards are what drive us all. Plan to celebrate your accomplishment with something special for each significant milestone you reach. (Just be sure it will be consistent with any wellness goals.) Try rewarding yourself right away after you reach your goal for the most significant increase in motivation. According to several studies, receiving a reward after achieving a goal boost motivational feeling.

FINDING SUPPORT SYSTEM AND ACCOUNTABILITY PARTNERS

What does being accountable mean? According to the definition, accountability is the characteristic or state of being willing or required to accept responsibility for one's acts.

Why is having or finding a running accountability partner important? Imagine the scene; You're standing at the starting line of a marathon you just signed up for. Who is beside you? Your closest friend, your spouse, or another relative? Or are you alone? Wouldn't having a running partner to support you through those challenging miles be wonderful? Please only respond if you're an elite runner. That is a joke because even professional runners train with accountability partners during the week.

A partner may push you further than you ever imagined you could go, which is what makes them so wonderful. No matter how far you want to run, a training buddy is a wonderful idea.

You should look for the following qualities in an accountability partner:

- They keep their word (They must show up when they say they will.)

- Accept accountability for their deeds (Be willing to discuss what went wrong)

- Address issues before they arise (two whiners won't get anything done; one of you needs to be a skilled problem solver).

How can you be good partners for each other now that you know what to look for?

- Specify your own running goal: Determine your individual running goals. Do you intend to participate in your first half-marathon in spring? Finding someone who shares your goals, well, that would be nice.

- Locate a trustworthy running partner: Maybe you're part of a jogging club in your area. Members may be in various phases. Identify the individual who consistently comes up and shares your ambition to reach the next level. You can find a running companion online if you are not part of a local running organization.

- Be honest with each other: You may have heard it's best to be honest. Running with negativity is one of the hardest things to accomplish.

Running is difficult enough, and we have many things to concentrate on. On occasion, it can be helpful to discuss personal difficulties while running. One of you can say, "I simply want to run today and talk about the positives in your life, not the negatives today," because honesty will allow that.

- Exercise together always: Set aside specific weekdays for your runs. It might only happen once a week. Make it excellent.

- Link responsibility with other aspects of your life: You might share goals beyond just running. Perhaps you both want to lose weight or are trying to save money for a memorable trip.

- Be the best accountability partner you can be: Be the change you want to see. We should bring dependability, honesty, and positivity into our relationship if we want it to succeed.

- Mix it up: Switching up your accountability partners is acceptable. You may have an accountability partner for long runs and another for faster, shorter runs. In the same way, there are several seasons and various needs for each. As time goes on, our needs could change.

Those are some recommendations for qualities to seek in an accountability partner. You can also use those suggestions to help someone else choose the best accountability partner.

HOW TO MAKE RUNNING A LIFESTYLE

Running doesn't have to be boring; it can be a fantastic opportunity to test your boundaries. Maintaining a sense of humor, gaining endurance gradually, and assembling a cheerleading squad can all help you turn running into a lifestyle rather than a difficult-to-maintain pastime.

Play it up!

Running should be enjoyable rather than work. The best motivation to keep running is to enjoy it. You can create your own game in various ways to keep it engaging. Choose several running locations and change the terrain using the trail, road, and track options to keep things interesting. Engage with your surroundings rather than just looking at the ground. As you run in the fall, count the pumpkins on porches. Running and walking between the mailboxes can give you pleasant exercise.

Listening to music or audiobooks can help you stay motivated during faster runs or get through the boring kilometers of a lengthy run. This is another approach to keep running enjoyable. If you decide to run plugged in, always be considerate and aware of your surroundings.

Develop your endurance

Marathoners don't go for their first run and complete a 20-mile distance. Never give up if you need to start with walking and running breaks to increase your endurance gradually. Every runner has to start somewhere. This simple approach boosts your endurance and mileage while lowering your risk of injury and burnout.

The walk breaks you take throughout your runs get shorter and farther between when you use the run/walk technique. For instance, if you start with a run-walk rhythm of four minutes of running and three minutes of walking, with time, the running portion will increase to five minutes, then six minutes, seven minutes, and eight minutes, while the walking portion will decrease to only a minute or two. You'll eventually be able to stop walking fully or limit your use of walk breaks when necessary.

Build a support group.

Getting out the door for a long run or a session in inclement weather is much easier if you have a running partner or group depending on you to be there. Join a local running club or bring a friend along for a few days a week of running so that you don't have an excuse to give up when the weather is poor or the snooze button appears appealing.

If you want to prepare for your first 5K, look for a race, choose a date, and let everyone know. Share your goals with your friends, family, and coworkers. You have a safety net of support to keep going and inspire you to strive high when you inform your loved ones about your training and progress. Knowing your loved ones will be at the finish line to witness you reach your goal is the best feeling when race day finally arrives.

Above all, remember that running is a privilege and a gift rather than a punishment.

CONCLUSION

This is a comprehensive manual that enables senior runners to take advantage of running without having to worry about getting injured. We have examined the particular difficulties elderly runners have throughout this book and have offered workable methods to address these difficulties and avoid injuries.

One of the most essential things in this book is that preventing injuries requires a comprehensive strategy incorporating several elements, such as healthy eating, enough hydration, stretching, strength training, and recuperation. By adopting these techniques into your running regimen, you may lessen the chance of injuries and continue to be healthy and active for years to come.

We have also learned how crucial paying attention to your body is. Our bodies change as we age, so modifying our workouts as necessary is essential. This entails being aware of the warning indicators, such as discomfort, stiffness, or exhaustion, and acting appropriately to alleviate them. Doing this may prevent overtraining and burnout and preserve a running schedule that promotes your health and well-being.

We've also discussed the advantages of cross-training, which is a fantastic method to supplement your running program and avoid injuries. Exercises that improve cardiovascular fitness, increase strength and flexibility, and lessen the pressure on your joints include cross-training exercises like cycling, swimming, and yoga. You can avoid boredom and maintain your drive by mixing up your workouts.

Finally, the significance of mindset in injury prevention has been highlighted in this book. Running involves both physical and mental activity. You can overcome challenges, maintain motivation, and enjoy the experience of running by taking a positive outlook. This entails establishing reasonable goals, acknowledging your successes, and being fair to yourself despite disappointments.

For anyone who wants to keep running far into their golden years, "Running Injury-Free for Runners Over 50" is a great resource. By using the tips and techniques in this book, you may lower your risk of injuries, maintain a healthy, active lifestyle, and get the numerous advantages of running, such as better cardiovascular health, reduced stress, and a sense of success.

Finally, injury prevention is a continuous effort that calls for dedication, endurance, and resilience. Even though it's not always easy, and you could have setbacks, you can get through them and keep improving as a runner with the appropriate attitude and techniques. Remember to cross-train, pay attention to your body, and keep a positive outlook. Above all, keep running injury-free, and have fun on the way!

References

A. (2021a, December 15). *Setting running goals for beginners: 6 Pro Tips*. Polar Journal. https://www.polar.com/blog/setting-running-goals/

ACE Physical Therapy and Sports Medicine Institute. (2020, December 22). *Benefits of Injury Prevention Programs Alexandria | Injuries Treatment Lansdowne*. https://ace-pt.org/benefits-injury-prevention-programs/

Carroll, C. (2021, February 26). *13 Key Training Tips for Older Runners*. Snacking in Sneakers. https://www.snackinginsneakers.com/training-tips-for-older-runners/

Chertoff, J. (2019, April 11). *What Are the Benefits of Foam Rolling?* Healthline. https://www.healthline.com/health/foam-roller-benefits

Clark, C. N. R. D. (2017, November 29). *How Aging Impacts Running Performance*. ACTIVE.com. https://www.active.com/running/Articles/How-Aging-Impacts-Running-Performance.htm?cmp=17-7-5492

Cronkleton, E. (2020, January 27). *How to Master Proper Running Form*. Healthline. https://www.healthline.com/health/exercise-fitness/proper-running-form

Crouch, S. (2015, August 7). *How to make running a lifestyle*. ACTIVE.com. https://www.active.com/running/articles/how-to-make-running-a-lifestyle

Cscs, K. V. D. O. (2021, July 29). *How to Start (and keep!) Running After Age 60*. Competitive Edge. https://compedgept.com/blog/running-after-sixty/

Dikos, R. J. D. (2020, September 17). *Fueling for Older Runners*. Runner's World.

https://www.runnersworld.com/advanced/a20798172/fueling-for-older-runners/

Fitzgerald, J. (2020, September 2). *Forget the 10% Rule: How to Increase Mileage Safely.* Strength Running. https://strengthrunning.com/2010/06/how-to-increase-mileage/

Gibala, M. J., Ph.D. (2017, November 27). *The Role of Protein in Exercise Recovery.* ACTIVE.com. https://www.active.com/nutrition/articles/the-role-of-protein-in-exercise-recovery

H. (2021b, June 15). *Combining your strength training and running.* The Hussle Blog. https://www.hussle.com/blog/combining-your-strength-training-and-running/

Harrington, M. (2022, December 27). *Hydration for Runners: Everything You Need to Know.* ACTIVE.com. https://www.active.com/running/articles/hydration-for-runners

How to Set Goals and Stay Motivated as a New Runner, according to a Running Coach. (2022, November 21). Very well Fit. https://www.verywellfit.com/beginner-runners-how-to-set-goals-and-stay-motivated-6828700

Intern, T. R., Bedosky, L., Kennedy, K., Fitzgerald, J., & Fitzgerald, J. (2017, July 31). *Stressed Out: How Stress Impacts Training and Performance.* Trail Runner Magazine. https://www.trailrunnermag.com/training/injuries-and-treatment-training/stressed-stress-impacts-training-performance/

LifeBridge Health. (2021, April 16). *Take it easy: How to gradually, and safely, approach running workouts after long periods of physical inactivity.* https://www.newswise.com/articles/take-it-easy-how-to-gradually-and-safely-approach-running-workouts-after-long-periods-of-physical-inactivity

Mateo, A. (2022, September 21). *Quick Fixes for the 15 Most Common Running Injuries.* Runner's World. https://www.runnersworld.com/health-injuries/a35994829/running-injuries/

Must-Do Strength Training Moves for Women Over 50. (2022, September 22). Verywell Fit. https://www.verywellfit.com/must-do-strength-training-women-over-50-3498202

New York Orthopedics. (2016, October 31). *Treatment Options for Common Running Injuries - Dr. Sergai DeLaMora*. NY Orthopedics. https://newyorkorthopedics.com/ny-orthopedics-doctors-highlights/treatment-options-common-running-injuries/

Norris, L. (2017, January 18). *Tempo and Interval Combo Workout*. Laura Norris Running. https://lauranorrisrunning.com/tempo-interval-combo-workout/

Parker, T. (2021, January 22). *#85 - 7 Tips for Running Accountability Partners w/ Chris Ballard & Katie Ayers*. Run to the Best You. https://www.runtothebestyou.com/news-notes/7-tips-for-running-accountability-partners-with-chris-ballard-and-katie-ayers

Polish, A. (2022, October 3). *How to Balance Running and Strength Training, No Matter Your Goals*. BarBend. https://barbend.com/running-and-strength-training/

R. (n.d.). *RECOVERY WITH AGING: HOW OLDER ADULTS SHOULD "RECOVER" FOLLOWING EXERCISE*. Recovapro. https://recovapro.co.uk/blogs/news/recovery-with-aging-how-older-adults-should-recover-following-exercise

Running Injury Rehabilitation | Missoula Sport and Orthopedic Physical Therapy. (n.d.). Endurance Physio Missoula Physical Therapy. https://www.endurancephysio.net/running-injury-rehabilitation-1

Sayer, A. (2022, November 18). *The Complete Runner' s Diet: What to Eat for Top Performance*. Marathon Handbook. https://marathonhandbook.com/the-complete-runners-diet-nutrition/

Should You Do Your Stretches Before and After Running? (2022, April 22). Verywell Fit. https://www.verywellfit.com/how-to-warm-up-and-cool-down-2911285

Sports Dietitians Australia. (2015, June 5). *Recovery Nutrition*. Sports Dietitians Australia (SDA). https://www.sportsdietitians.com.au/factsheets/fuelling-recovery/recovery-nutrition/

Strength Running. (2021, March 18). *Mental Toughness for Runners: The Ultimate Guide*. https://strengthrunning.com/mental-toughness-for-runners/

The Runner's World Editors. (2022, March 3). *41 Superfoods: How They Can Help Your Running*. Runner's World. https://www.runnersworld.com/nutrition-weight-loss/g20836777/41-superfoods-how-they-can-help-your-running/

Tocci, K. (2022, November 17). *Base Training for Runners: The Complete Guide*. Marathon Handbook. https://marathonhandbook.com/base-training-for-runners/

Why Sleep Is Key for Injury Prevention and Pain Management. (2022, January 13). https://www.risescience.com/blog/injury-prevention

Wr, T. (2020, April 16). *Do Runners Need More Antioxidants in Their Diets?* Women's Running. https://www.womensrunning.com/health/food/runners-antioxidants-diets/

Z. (2018, March 12). *7 Bad Running Technique Habits, And How to Avoid Them*. We Run UK. https://we-run.co.uk/good-running-technique-7-bad-running-form-habits-and-how-to-avoid-them/

Printed in Great Britain
by Amazon